THE
ADVANCED
DRIVER'S
HANDBOOK

THE
ADVANCED
DRIVER'S
HANDBOOK

NIGEL & MARGARET STACEY

Illustrated by Andy Rice

Published in association with
RoSPA

**KOGAN
PAGE**

First published in Great Britain in 1988
by Kogan Page Limited
120 Pentonville Road, London N1 9JN

Copyright © Nigel Stacey, Margaret Stacey and Andrew Rice 1988

Reprinted 1988

British Library Cataloguing in Publication Data
  Data is available.

  ISBN 1-85091-325-0

Printed and bound in Great Britain by
Biddles Ltd, Guildford, Surrey

Contents

Foreword

The RoSPA Advanced Drivers Association was the first organisation of its kind to be formed in the United Kingdom and was almost certainly also the first in the world outside the United States of America. Then known as the League of Safe Drivers, it was formed in 1955 by a group of instructors at the Metropolitan Police Driving School, Hendon. One of the first patrons was the local MP, a comparatively little-known lady: Mrs Margaret Thatcher!

The purpose of the organisation is to improve driving generally by the spread of knowledge about the police system of car control. Today this system is exported all over the world by both the police and the Royal Society for the Prevention of Accidents. In 1980 the League of Safe Drivers became part of RoSPA, the largest safety organisation in Europe. Its name was changed and it is now called the RoSPA Advanced Drivers Association. The league has benefited considerably by being part of RoSPA. It has moved into a new era and is now recognised as one of, if not the, premier 'advanced driving' organisation.

Director of Road Safety
RoSPA

About the Guide and its Authors

This guide is part of a series of interrelated projects which have evolved in response to general demands for improved driving standards. The concept was developed by a small group of instructors and consultants who have influenced standards of driving at home and abroad. It combines established advanced and economy driving skills with defensive driving techniques.

The guide is designed to make readers more aware of the locations at which accidents occur, the mistakes which precede them and the actions needed to prevent them. Emphasis is on hazard awareness and self-control. The visual techniques help readers to predict potential danger earlier and so avoid the conflict which leads to road accidents.

Nigel Stacey is co-author of *The Driving Instructor's Handbook* and author of *Running Your Own Driving School*. He played an important part in restructuring the staff tutor courses of the National Joint Council and was instrumental in developing the syllabus for the *Diploma in Driving Instruction*.

Margaret and Nigel Stacey are co-authors of *Learn to Drive*, a new kind of structured learning guide for provisional licence holders. This is graphically illustrated by Andy Rice to support professional instruction and between lesson practice. It identifies key learning points and reinforces them with a Highway Code self-learning and testing programme.

The authors have developed a new kind of visual teaching system which provides instructors and road safety officers with support for a wide range of pre-driver, defensive and vocational courses.

Introduction

Road accidents — The biggest epidemic of our time

Every year accidents kill over 5,000 road users and seriously injure another 300,000 in the UK. This is approximately equivalent to exploding a Hiroshima-sized atom bomb over a small town somewhere in Britain every year. The cost to the community is over £2,500 million per year or £288,000 per hour. Every day 14 men, women and children die from road accidents caused by lack of attention, deficient driving skills and impairment. Every hour, 30 people are seriously injured, many of them children under the age of six.

Why accidents happen

TRRL Supplementary Report 567, *The Known Risks We Run on the Highway*, by Barbara E Sabey and H Taylor, identifies the contributory factors involved in road accidents.

Vehicle defects contribute to about 8% of all accidents

These vehicle defects and other factors include:
tyres (3.3%); brakes (3.2%); steering (0.34%); lights (0.49%); mechanical failure (1%); electrical failure (0.2%); loads (0.49%); windscreen (0.2%); bad visibility (0.2%); overall poor condition (0.25%); unsuitable design (0.44%).

Adverse road environment contributes to about 28% of all accidents

Adverse environment includes factors relating to:

Adverse road design (15.5%):
- unsuitable layout or junction design
- poor visibility due to layout.

Adverse environment (13.8%):
- slippery road or flooded surface
- lack of maintenance
- weather conditions or dazzle.

Inadequate furniture or markings (7.7%):
- inadequate signs
- worn road markings
- street lighting.

Obstructions (6.3%):
- road works
- parked vehicles or other objects.

Human error contributes to about 95% of all road accidents

Human error includes factors relating to:

Perception (56%):
● lack of concentration
● failure to see or recognise the risk
● misjudgement of speed or distance.

Lack of skill (22%):
● inexperience
● lack of judgement
● incorrect actions or decisions.

Manner of execution (66%):
● excessive speed
● unsafe overtaking
● failure to look
● following too closely
● irresponsible, reckless, frustrated or aggressive behaviour.

Impairment (31%):
● alcohol
● fatigue
● drugs
● illness
● emotional distress.

Factors influencing driver behaviour

THE PRINCIPLE OF LIVING AND ACTING FOR THE GOOD OF OTHERS.

In Britain the traditional approach to advanced driving is based on altruism. This implies that safe drivers require an attitude of mind that embodies consideration for the rights and *safety of others*. Whilst few people would dispute the desirability of these qualities, the behaviour of individuals is seldom governed by altruistic motives.

This suggests that safe drivers are those who have an attitude of mind which preserves *their own safety*. You should continually be considering the actions and potential actions of others and should drive prepared to compensate for their mistakes.

Attitudes are formed by the interaction of your total experiences from birth and your personality. They reflect the manner in which you respond to people, things, situations and problems. Judgements are influenced by attitudes assumed in advance, which tend to make you see things not as they actually are, but as you imagine them. Furthermore, due to motivational and emotional elements, a driver's attitude can suddenly change from one of consideration to outright hostility.

Motivation describes your personal needs and drives. These are directed to survival, wellbeing and achieving the fulfilment of your personal desires. Motivation can sometimes manifest itself in unusual ways: for example, a driver may take risks that he might otherwise find unacceptable

- if late for work or an important appointment
- to get the better of the driver of the sports car that just passed him
- to demonstrate the superiority of skills and/or to gain the admiration of friends of the opposite sex, or peers, or self.

Emotion is the term used to describe states of feeling such as love, hate and fear. Intense emotions like anger, frustration and grief tend to focus the attention of the mind upon itself. This can lower your attention on driving and limit the perceptive abilities of your mind. Anger may be the result of an argument with a wife or husband, frustration may be the result of being held up behind a slow moving vehicle, anxiety may be the result of worries about work or an important appointment.

Personality is described as the outcome of inherited potentialities modified by experience. Our perception of ourselves is different from our personality as it is perceived by others. The overt personality that we display to others is rarely the same as that perceived within our own private consciousness. There is evidence to suggest that extrovert drivers are more likely to be involved in accidents than introvert drivers. This may be linked to an inability to concentrate for long periods of time.

Knowledge is assumed to influence attitudes and assist in the acquisition of driving skills. Knowledge of the latest Highway Code rules and regulations, together with an understanding of critical events leading up to accidents, will help drivers to recognise risk and respond to it sooner.

Physical and mental impairment

Alcohol
Alcohol is a drug and a contributory factor in over 30% of road accidents. After just one drink a driver is less able to make decisions quickly and react promptly in an emergency.

After the second drink a driver will become more relaxed, with less concern for normal restraint and attention to detail. There is a further deterioration in mental responses and physical reactions, combined with a slight degeneration in co-ordination and the execution of manipulative skills.

After a third drink a driver's emotions become more extreme and behaviour exaggerated. The driver becomes more confident, talkative, noisy or morose and there is a further deterioration in reactions, co-ordination and manipulative skill. Perceptive responses become slower and impossible feats are far more likely to be attempted.

After the fourth drink there is still further deterioration in co-ordination to the point of clumsiness. Confidence continues to increase whilst perceptive skills are unknowingly deteriorating. The driver's levels of attention and powers of discrimination and normal restraint are rapidly disappearing. Impossible feats are even more likely to be attempted.

After the fifth drink normal perception of moving and static objects becomes blurred. It takes longer for the eyes to focus, and speeds and distances are severely misjudged. The driver's ability to make sensible decisions, and react promptly, is totally unreliable, resulting in high accident-risk manoeuvres being unknowingly attempted.

Non-alcoholic drugs

Drugs impair driving ability by reducing attention levels, the perception of risk, and the ability to make sound decisions quickly and respond promptly to the road and traffic scene. Studies in the USA show that about 10% of drivers involved in accidents take non-alcoholic drugs of some kind.

Drivers suffering from some temporary illness should be advised to ask their doctors whether any prescribed drugs they are taking will affect their driving ability. Read instructions on the labels of non-prescribed drugs.

Amphetamines speed up the nervous system and help users to 'keep going'. Whilst taking this type of drug, users may feel more alert and confident, but, when the effect wears off, they are likely to feel very tired and depressed.

Barbiturates are used to calm the nerves. They have an effect similar to that of alcohol, but when the effect wears off depression may follow. A combination of barbiturates and alcohol can cause severe depression. Tranquillisers are used by people with nervous and emotional conditions. They cause drowsiness and are often combined with alcohol, with severe or even fatal consequences.

Marijuana is a hallucinogen which can act as either a stimulant or depressant. It slows mental responses and physical reactions; affects the judgement of time and space; and limits the ability to concentrate on more than one thing at a time.

Fatigue

Fatigue is a temporary condition that impairs the ability of all drivers. It reduces the ability to concentrate, impairs vision and the other senses, makes decisions more difficult and the driver more irritable and so less tolerant of other road users.

Fatigue can be caused by hard work, lack of rest, emotional stress, boredom or carbon monoxide poisoning. Contributory factors may include illness, over-eating, an overheated car, driving for long distances without rest, bright sunlight or glare from oncoming headlights.

Carbon monoxide is discharged by the car's exhaust system. If this is leaking, if boot seals are not effective, or if the tailgate of an estate or hatchback car is not fully closed, carbon monoxide may find its way into the passenger compartment. It is colourless, odourless, tasteless and poisonous. Keep plenty of fresh air circulating through the car.

Emotions and stress

Extreme emotions, such as fear or anger, affect attention levels, perception and response to everyday traffic situations. They limit the driver's ability to reason quickly and logically.

Driving is stressful in itself. High levels of frustration are created by the vehicle and traffic environment. Stress can cause excessive overreaction which adds even more fuel to the fire. On the other hand these overreactions may (particularly in the case of new drivers in situations they are not yet competent to deal with) be associated with poorly developed hazard recognition skills, resulting in additional stresses due to late reactions and lack of confidence due to deficient car control skills.

Aggression is characterised by the hostile feelings or behaviour which some drivers display towards others. Normal, mentally healthy people are able to tolerate a degree of aggression towards themselves without retaliation. Some experts claim aggression is linked to one individual's desire to dominate another and to compensate for feelings of inferiority or inadequacy. Others describe it as a surge of destructive feeling provoked by frustration. It is unlikely that aggression can be completely suppressed and where it manifests itself in driving, it should be directed towards the error being committed rather than the person committing it.

Young people are generally more at risk because they are less able to control hostile feelings. However, aggressive behaviour is not restricted to any particular age group or gender if a driver is pushed beyond his limits.

Illness
Everyone suffers from temporary minor illnesses from time to time, such as colds, toothaches, headaches and tummy upsets. The effect of these can be to reduce attention, impair vision and upset judgements, timing and co-ordination.

Ageing
Ageing can reduce perception and impair manipulative co-ordination. Older people are more set in their ways and will generally find learning to drive more difficult. They tend to be more anxious and their reactions are generally slower.

Temporary physical interference
The use of microphones, car telephones and CB radios is a serious distraction to driving. Drivers should not use hand-held microphones or telephone handsets whilst the vehicle is moving, except in an emergency. They should only use fixed, neckslung or clipped-on microphones when it would not distract their attention from the road and traffic situation. (It is argued that any serious conversation is a distraction.)

The problems caused can be alleviated by the more sensible use of such equipment. It is safest to use it only when the vehicle is standing. It is advisable that calls are not answered nor put out when in motion and that any serious conversations are suspended until a suitable parking place can be found.

There are many other similar activities which reduce the driver's attention on the road and traffic scene: for example, unrelated physical actions such as lighting a cigarette, tuning the car radio, looking for maps or papers, winding the window down, or mental activity such as serious conversation or argument with passengers or looking for a street name or house number.

Perceptual motor skills

This is a complex set of interacting perceptive and manipulative skills. They are executed partly consciously and partly subconsciously. The driving task involves *attending*, *perceiving*, and *responding* safely to relevant stimulae. You must first obtain relative information from the environment, process it and then respond by making decisions and carrying out the appropriate car control skills. These skills include:
- *attention* to the driving task
- *systematic visual search* of the road and traffic environment and identifying and awarding priorities for/to relevant cues
- *assessing* the potential risk of accidents
- *anticipating* possible and subsequent events

- *deciding* upon appropriate actions
- *responding* in a restrained manner: by communicating with others; by executing controlled changes in speed and/or position; and with further observation of the situation and continual re-assessment.

Attention to the driving task

Attention can either be divided over the whole traffic scene or focused selectively on specific areas or objects of particular interest. Selective attention requires more effort and can only be sustained for short periods. High levels of conscious attention are difficult for anyone to sustain for periods in excess of 20 minutes.

A characteristic of advanced drivers is that they learn how to allocate and distribute their attention to maximise the useful information they obtain about road and traffic hazards. A hazard is anything containing an element of risk or potential risk that causes you concern or to consider changes in your direction and/or speed. For example:

- physical features such as bends, junctions and hillcrests
- blind areas of road, footpath or relevant nearby areas
- movement or potential movement of others into or across your path
- road surface condition and other factors affecting stability or adhesion.

Actual hazards incur risk factors which are easily seen and identified. Most drivers are prepared to act when they recognise, for example, a pedestrian running across the road. Potential hazards tend to be more difficult to recognise. They incur risk factors which are less easily seen, difficult to identify and sometimes hard to accept. They include the potential for movement across your path, restricted sightlines behind parked vehicles and factors affecting vehicle stability.

Not only must drivers recognise the obvious risk caused by a child running out into the road, but also the less obvious risk that the child standing on the pavement may run out, or the even less obvious risk of the unseen child who may run out from behind a parked vehicle.

Perception is your brain's interpretation of information provided by your eyes, ears and other senses. It involves comparisons with existing knowledge and previous experience. Numerous research studies show that all drivers have limited perceptual capacities, yet we are frequently faced with an overload of information from the vehicle, road and traffic environment. Traffic hazards rarely occur in isolation. You must attend to and identify other risk factors in different parts of the road. In these situations we make a decision to attend to some of the available information and reject or ignore other aspects of it. All drivers should recognise that this discrepancy exists between the task demands and their own capabilities and that it can be reduced by appropriate reductions in speed.

Visual search skills

Your eyes are naturally attracted to movement, bright colours and unusual happenings. Not all are relevant to particular road and traffic situations. You therefore require an effective system of visual scanning to maximise the input of useful information.

You should look and plan well ahead in order to steer a safe and smooth line and make early adjustments to speeds in response to possible obstructions, road geometry and traffic signs. You should continually look for situations containing a potential for other road users to move into or turn across your course, and areas of restricted vision which may be hiding other road users moving into or turning across your course. Work out in advance what action you will take if events change.

Assessing risk

Driving is a continuous process of attending to, perceiving and responding to constantly changing needs involving the vehicle, the road layout and traffic conditions. You must continually check, assess and re-assess the hazards and the responses you are making to them. You should:

- look, assess, and decide what action can safely be taken relating to information received from the *mirrors*; decide if a *signal* is necessary;
- look, assess, and decide whether a *signal* is having the required effect on the actions of following traffic;
- look, assess, and decide what effect any changes in *position and speed* are likely to have or are having on other road users; and decide what further *looks* may be required.

There is some connection between safe driver behaviour and your own personal assessment of the potential risk levels of being involved in an accident. Your assessment of the risk will be influenced by previous experience. Assessing risks and deciding on the appropriate response to a traffic hazard involves a continuous re-circulating chain of checking, re-checking, assessing and re-assessing the

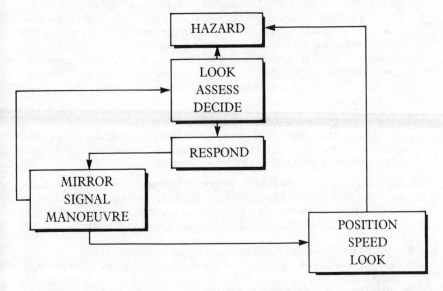

Figure 1 *Driving is a continuous process of assessment and reassessment*

constantly changing environment. It involves:

- assessing the degree of risk involved in the hazard
- awarding priorities to the hazard in relation to the whole traffic scene
- directing further attention to it
- deciding on a specific course of action
- responding by signalling intentions and/or maintaining or changing speed and/or position
- creating time for the situation to change and/or to obtain additional information about the situation before re-assessing.

Anticipation

Anticipation is your ability to predict the actions of other road users. This skill is related to risk assessment and they are often jointly called the hazard recognition skills. Anticipation is also closely linked to the visual search skills and involves attaching meaning to driving-relevant cues. You should know:

- what to expect and the kind of things you should look for
- why, where and when you should look hardest
- how to look and visually scan the road effectively.

Making decisions

Many drivers are indecisive and then make rash decisions on the spur of the moment. One major problem seems to be that they make decisions before they have sufficient information on which to base them. Such decisions frequently polarise between 'stop and go' where neither are correct, for example where action is needed to provide *time* to allow the situation to develop and/or obtain more information. Inadequate information and hurried assessments are a major cause of incorrect decisions. This stop–go approach is characteristic of those who make decisions which result in high accident risk. For example: there are three possible decisions to be made when approaching a stationary car parked on the left 300 yards ahead with a stream of slow moving traffic approaching from the opposite direction. These are:

1. It is safe to proceed or to carry out an intended manoeuvre.
2. It is unsafe at the moment to proceed or to execute an intended manoeuvre.
3. More information is needed to assess the situation or more time is required to permit development before a decision can be made.

Any decision to proceed, hold back, give way, wait or stop must be continually re-assessed. For choices 2 and 3 the response is nearly always the same and will be to delay the ultimate manoeuvre either until circumstances permit or sufficient information has been obtained to make a decision to proceed. This can be done by:

- slowing down and making time for the situation to develop;
- slowing down to obtain more information about the potential movement of pedestrians;
- obtaining more information about the presence or potential presence of any oncoming vehicles;

- reviewing the changed situation after and as a result of slowing down;
- improving the view by changes in lateral position and/or 'feeling' the way forward cautiously.

Work things out in advance! For example, approaching a green traffic light, anticipate the possibility of it changing and be ready with the decision to stop. At some point on the approach, however, you will be too close to pull up safely. Once you reach and cross this point the only decision you can make is to continue. Continually re-assess what you will do if the lights change. The decisions can be made in advance leaving the response to be triggered by the event.

Car control skills

Many drivers wrongly assess the quality of their own driving performance from their manipulative skills in car control alone. Whilst they are important, the perceptive skills are more significant in the prevention of accidents.

The manipulative skills involve your ability to communicate with other road users, regulate speed, steer and position safely and maintain adequate safety margins. Emergency handling techniques involve your ability to perform evasive actions in emergencies and regain proper control with adequate safety margins.

After carrying out the look/assess/decide routine and starting a course of action to proceed, wait or delay progress to obtain more information before making a commitment, the driver will respond with the routine procedures.

Mirror: Apply the look/assess/decide routine to the mirror and consider how the information obtained from it will affect the intended actions.

Signals: Methods of communication between road users are complex and much broader than traditional signals, such as: direction indicators; arm signals to other road users; stop light signals; arm signals to traffic controllers; horn; flashing headlights and the hazard warning flasher. Road users also communicate intentions and courtesies using:

- the speed of a vehicle;
- the lateral and forward position of a vehicle along the road;
- implied signals of intent (linked to movement/position of pedestrians);
- eye contact with other road users; and
- courtesy signals and acknowledgements of other road users.

Manoeuvre: The manoeuvre consists of the position, speed, look routine. Suffice to say it is anything involving changes in speed or direction. It is normally always preceded and followed by the continuous process of looking, assessing and deciding.

Position and Speed: Your awareness and judgement of position and speed should be linked. As speed is increased, your point of focus will get further ahead with a corresponding reduction in your peripheral sensitivity. Where you need to attend to foreground detail, speed must be reduced. Peripheral vision also helps you judge your speed and position. Failure to reduce speed will result in important risk factors being ignored and reduced awareness of lateral positions and safety margins.

Look: Last, but by no means least, back to where the whole process of attending – assessing, deciding and responding – started.

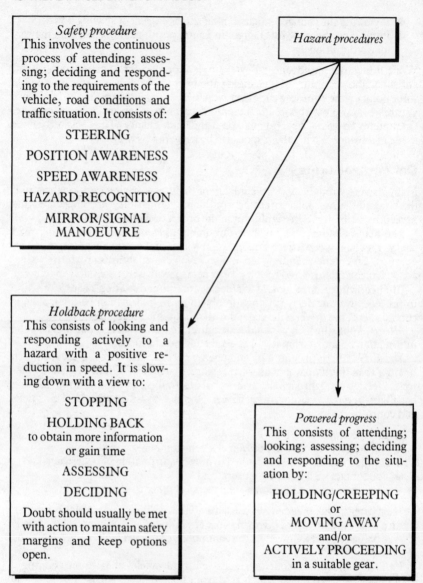

Safety procedure
This involves the continuous process of attending; assessing; deciding and responding to the requirements of the vehicle, road conditions and traffic situation. It consists of:

STEERING

POSITION AWARENESS

SPEED AWARENESS

HAZARD RECOGNITION

MIRROR/SIGNAL
MANOEUVRE

Hazard procedures

Holdback procedure
This consists of looking and responding actively to a hazard with a positive reduction in speed. It is slowing down with a view to:

STOPPING

HOLDING BACK
to obtain more information
or gain time

ASSESSING

DECIDING

Doubt should usually be met with action to maintain safety margins and keep options open.

Powered progress
This consists of attending; looking; assessing; deciding and responding to the situation by:

HOLDING/CREEPING
or
MOVING AWAY
and/or
ACTIVELY PROCEEDING
in a suitable gear.

Figure 2 *Driving involves assessing and responding correctly to driving-relevant stimuli*

1 Understanding Road Accidents

Could you prevent this accident?

Accidents are defined as 'events without cause'. Over 90% of road accidents, however, are *caused by human error*. They are also caused by 'unexpected events' and false assumptions. Some drivers who fail to consider unexpected, but nevertheless predictable, events put themselves and others at risk. To assume can make an 'ass' out of 'u' and 'me'.

The long-term answer to road accidents lies in increased hazard awareness, the ability to predict unexpected events, and the preparedness to compensate. The accident about to happen below could be prevented if only any one of the three drivers involved were more aware.

The driver turning into the main road is looking to his right for traffic and not expecting vehicles approaching along his side of the road. *If only* he were to look both ways before emerging . . .

Vehicles parked near junctions restrict vision and put drivers on to the wrong side of the road. Some drivers park without consideration for anyone else, as long as it is convenient for them. Others just don't think or don't know the rules! *If only* the driver of the parked vehicle had selected a safer place to leave it . . .

The driver moving out to pass the parked vehicle 'assumed' anyone approaching the junction would stop. He has failed to predict the possibility of the vehicle emerging and is travelling too fast to pull up. *If only* he was aware of the potential danger he would slow down and so be able to stop . . .

If only . . .

Most accidents are preventable!

No matter whose fault or 'right of way' it may be, collisions cause inconvenience, injury, and misery to those involved.

Accidents take lives! They are costly and may mean disqualification, losing your job and financial hardship.

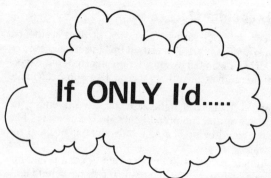

The consequences of excess speed

Many people drive dangerously fast at the wrong time, in the wrong place and under the wrong conditions. This is often because they fail to recognise the risks involved and do not slow down when the circumstances change.

Show consideration to other road users by driving at a speed at which you are able to pull up comfortably and well within the distance you know is clear.

Because you are driving within the legal limit does not mean your speed is safe for the conditions!

Anticipate the mistakes of other road users

Can you recall the near misses you've experienced because someone unexpectedly moved into your path? Think about the consequences of an oncoming car turning across your path, or of a cyclist pulling out into the road. Could you stop if a pedestrian suddenly ran out from behind a parked vehicle?

Are you fit to drive?

Can you still read a number plate from at least 67 feet away? If you need glasses to do this, you must wear them for driving!

Ask your doctor if any medicines or drugs prescribed will affect your driving.

Alcohol is a major cause of road accidents. It is also a drug and even small amounts will impair your perception of danger. It blurs your judgement of speeds and distance and your reactions will be slower.

If you drink heavily the night before, the amount of alcohol in your body may still exceed the legal limit in the morning.

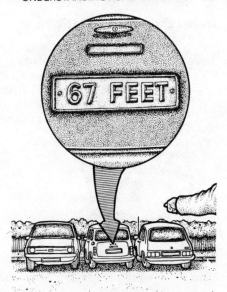

Reduce distractions when driving

It's a good idea to visit the toilet before a journey. If you become uncomfortable whilst driving it will be harder to concentrate.

Avoid arguments before and whilst driving as they put you in the wrong frame of mind and make it harder to concentrate.

Most serious accidents happen within five miles of home! This may be due to over-familiarity with local roads and concentration being low at the start of a journey or relaxing towards the end.

Delay the onset of fatigue

Wear light, comfortable and loose-fitting clothes. Heavy or tight-fitting coats may restrict steering and body movement. Wear flat shoes with enclosed or covered heels. Heavy boots and fashion shoes are normally unsuited and make control difficult.

Make sure you're comfortable! Aches and pains are distractions and haste the onset of fatigue.

Before driving an unfamiliar car, get used to the position and feel of the controls.

Position your right foot so that you can pivot quickly between the accelerator and brake pedal.

To test the seat position ensure you can push the clutch to the floor without stretching. Most drivers sit too close! This causes erratic steering and makes it awkward to control the pedals.

Sit up with your bottom well back in the seat and make sure you can see clearly. Remove any stickers or toy mascots which may restrict your view.

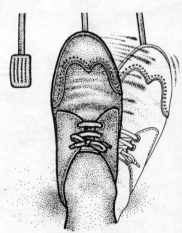

Reduce passenger-related risks

Opening a car door carelessly can put you or your passengers in danger and may force others to brake or swerve. Open the door, place your left foot on to the floor and sit down on the seat. Swing your right foot in quickly and close the door. Listen to make sure passengers close theirs and check that the handbrake is firmly on. Ask your passengers to get in from the footpath side and sit where they don't restrict your view in the mirror.

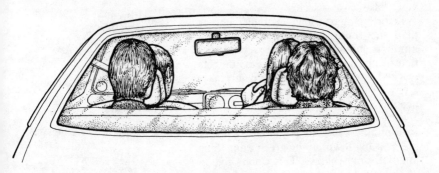

Adjust the mirrors so you can see clearly to the rear with the minimum of head movement. Line up the top edge of the mirror along the top edge of the rear window, and the offside edge (driver's side) of the rear window down its right side. Adjust the door mirrors to reduce the blind areas at your sides.

Concentrating for long periods is tiring. You will need plenty of fresh air to stay alert. Keep the in-car temperature comfortable, but not too warm. A slightly open window will keep the air circulating and prevent condensation forming on the windows in cold weather, particularly with a car full of passengers.

Make sure passengers wear seatbelts and carry children only in the rear. Fasten small ones in approved harnesses or child seats. Put the child locks on so the doors can't be opened from inside. Children get bored quickly and may distract you; make sure they are restrained and that animals are kept under proper control.

Plan your journey

Three-quarters of the drivers involved in collisions are within ten miles of home when the accident occurs. Perhaps the fact that they are going to be late for work, tired at the end of a hard day, frustrated by traffic holdups, thinking about what they're going to do that evening, or worrying about family problems may be contributory factors.

Concentrate wherever you are and try not to let your familiarity with local roads give you a false sense of security.

Before going on a long unfamiliar journey plan the route and jot down the road numbers and towns along the way. Make a note of any motorways and the exit numbers marked on the map. A route card only takes a few minutes to prepare and reduces the need for in-car map reading.

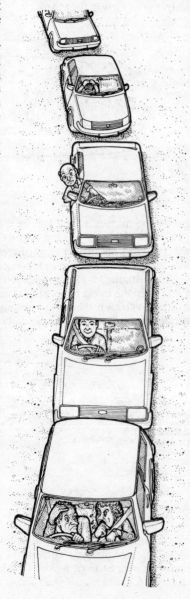

As you drive along, look out for major road numbers like the A1 and the name of the next big town on the green signs (blue for motorway routes). This colour coding helps you pick out the sign you have to follow more easily. Less important routes and local direction signs have a white background.

On journeys, have you ever noticed that once things start to go wrong, nothing seems to go right? The later you get, the more other people seem to get in your way. Everyone seems to be crawling and all the traffic lights are on red!

Start your journey early! This enables you to concentrate on your driving and avoid the frustration and anxiety which can build up through holdups and diversions.

Once you become late it gets more difficult to concentrate; the later you become the more risks you will take! If you get behind schedule, remember, it is far better to arrive late and composed for an important business appointment than not to get there at all!

Be tolerant with those less skilful than yourself

How well do you know your Highway Code? An up-to-date understanding of the procedures helps you work out what others are doing, recognise danger sooner and react more quickly and decisively. Knowledgeable drivers are more confident and relaxed; they are usually more tolerant and less likely to get frustrated by the mistakes of others. Less easily provoked by bad manners, they are unlikely to respond aggressively.

Be patient with those less skilful than yourself! Some drivers have a completely wrong attitude to road driving. They are aggressive, inconsiderate, quick to lose their tempers and a major cause of accidents.

Aggressive behaviour can create stress. It could force others to act involuntarily and cause them to lose control.

An unsound decision, made under pressure, could kill!

Keep calm and ignore impatient drivers. Let them wait until *you* are completely sure it is safe to proceed.

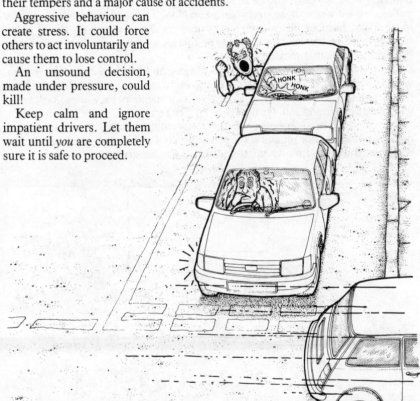

Reduce breakdowns and roadside repairs

Nearly one vehicle in every ten involved in accidents has a defect which is completely responsible or contributes to its cause. Have your vehicle properly serviced and maintained. This will reduce the risk of prosecution or being involved in an accident due to mechanical failure, and lessen the chances of breaking down.

Looking through scratched or dirty windows is tiring and causes glare from bright sunlight and the headlights of oncoming vehicles. This can cause momentary blindness and be painful to the eyes. Use water and a soft cloth or leather to regularly wash windows and clean the mirrors and lights.

Before a journey walk around your car and look for any obvious defects such as loose trims, number plates or exhausts hanging down. Check for flat or badly worn tyres and ensure the indicators and lights are working. The footbrake should be checked soon after moving away.

If you should break down on the road, always think of others and try to get your vehicle off the main highway. If you are on a motorway, get on to the hard shoulder and phone for help. If the emergency telephones are out of order stay with your vehicle and wait for the special police patrols.

Switch your hazard flashers on and erect a warning triangle if you have one. Do not attempt any major repairs at the roadside and if you need to carry out a minor repair think about your own safety and that of passing drivers.

Avoid distractions in the car

Before driving away, look around for loose articles which might distract you. Tidy up maps, papers or other things lying about.

If they fall about when accelerating, slowing down or cornering they could distract you and cause you to have an accident.

Make sure there is nothing on the floor likely to roll around, such as a child's ball. Apart from being a distraction, if an aerosol can or other object rolls under the pedals it may prevent the brakes from being applied.

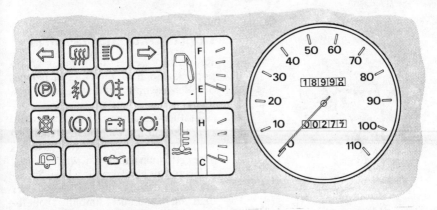

Instrument checks

Ignoring warning lights can result in breakdowns or serious damage. Check that the battery charging and oil pressure warning lights operate as you start the engine. They should normally go out as soon as it is running.

When driving, glance at one instrument at a time. Do this quickly when there is nothing happening in the road ahead. Stop in a safe position and get help if a malfunction occurs with the braking system, if your engine becomes overheated or the oil pressure warning light comes on.

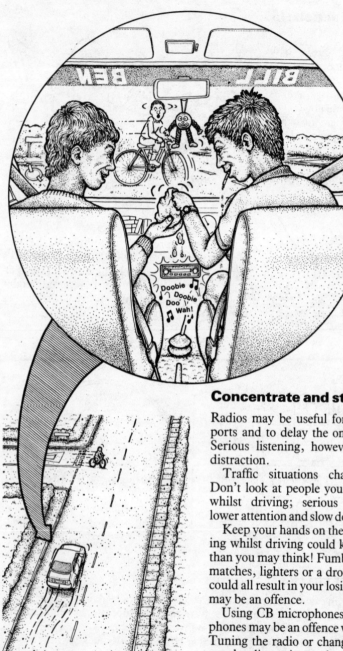

Concentrate and stay alive

Radios may be useful for motoring reports and to delay the onset of fatigue. Serious listening, however, may be a distraction.

Traffic situations change quickly. Don't look at people you are talking to whilst driving; serious conversations lower attention and slow down reactions.

Keep your hands on the wheel. Smoking whilst driving could kill you sooner than you may think! Fumbling about for matches, lighters or a dropped cigarette could all result in your losing control and may be an offence.

Using CB microphones or radio telephones may be an offence whilst driving. Tuning the radio or changing a cassette are also distractions to be avoided on the move and especially when driving at speed or in traffic.

2 High Performance Handling Techniques

Factors affecting the stability of vehicles in motion

Friction provides the only control drivers have over the direction and speed of their vehicles. If the forces placed on the vehicle exceed the friction between the tyre and road surface, the vehicle will go out of control. The importance of friction, and other factors involved in maintaining stability, are not always properly understood by many drivers. They include:

- adhesive characteristics of tyres such as:
  - state of wear
  - design factors
  - pressure
  - rubber compounds used; together with the
- grip coefficient of the road surface:
  - state of repair and condition
  - presence of surface lubricants such as water, oil, rubber dust, melting rubber, mud and loose grit
- inertia – the natural resistance of a moving mass to changes in its state of rest or uniform motion;
- gravity – holding the vehicle on the road and keeping the tyres in contact with the surface
  - applying acceleration and braking forces on hills
  - deflecting vehicle direction on cambered roads, particularly at speed on curves with adverse cambers
- efficiency of the suspension system in coping with the effects of inertia:
  - over uneven surfaces
  - on curved paths
  - when braking and accelerating
  - and to prevent the tyres becoming airborne
  - over bumps and hollows
  - when cornering
  - when changing speed
- the speed of the vehicle; and
  - the lift forces being generated.

Partial or complete contact may be lost due to: a combination of excess speed on an uneven or bumpy road; an inadequate suspension system or faults in it.

Adhesion may be lost due to the tyres riding above the surface on a cushion of water, oil or other unstable material; excessive acceleration, braking and cornering forces exerted, causing the rubber compound of the tyre to melt and form a thin film of lubricant on top of the road surface.

Vehicle steering characteristics

Centrifugal force and other factors contribute to reducing the stability of a vehicle when it is negotiating a curved path. The tyres and suspension system are designed to optimise the grip on the road surface and control the natural effect of these forces. The weight distribution of loads and passengers in a car and the layout of the engine and transmission affect the steering. Due to the position of the engine and transmission, front wheel drive vehicles carry the weight at the front and consequently tend to understeer with the natural stability of a dart. Vehicles with their engine/transmission systems at the rear tend to oversteer and they are naturally unstable.

Understeer handling characteristics are designed into most modern cars to improve stability when cornering and driving at speed in crosswinds. Understeering describes the tendency for the vehicle to run wide on a curved path. It is simply countered by a slight increase in the degree of steering lock needed to negotiate the bend. Mild understeer provides good directional stability and is less demanding. Excessive understeer makes a vehicle unresponsive to the driver's efforts with the wheel. This can make driving hard work in towns and on winding country roads. Neutral steering characteristics or mild oversteer makes the steering more responsive.

Oversteer reduces a vehicle's stability, particularly when driving at higher speeds and when cornering. Oversteer vehicles are directionally unstable and require frequent steering corrections, particularly in strong crosswinds, when driving at speed, and on roads with pronounced changes in camber. Oversteer is the tendency for the vehicle to point itself into a bend more than anticipated from the steering wheel movement. It is countered by slight decreases in the degree of steering used.

The over- and understeer characteristics may change as speed is increased. For example: a car which normally understeers can, as the speed increases, develop neutral steer and then oversteer. To be controllable these changes must be progressive and predictable otherwise they can catch a driver unawares and prove very dangerous.

The over- and understeer characteristics of a vehicle may change according to accelerator pressures. Releasing the accelerator of a front wheel drive car transfers weight onto the front wheels and increases the cornering force they exert on the road surface. A naturally oversteering vehicle can snake about quite violently if hard acceleration is used on a corner or bend.

Slip angles. When steering round a bend, the tyres point in a slightly different direction to the course of the vehicle and it is the difference between the direction of tyre travel and the plane of the wheel that is called the slip angle. Where the slip angles of the front tyres are greater than those at the rear the vehicle understeers. Conversely, where the slip angles at the rear are greater than those at the front, the vehicle oversteers. Radial tyres have smaller slip angles than crossply tyres. It is illegal to fit radial tyres to the front wheels when crossply are fitted to the rear because it will create an oversteer characteristic and cause directional instability.

Roadholding and handling characteristics. These are usually a compromise between the ride and handling characteristics built into the vehicle. The ride describes the smoothed-out motion experienced by the occupants after the insulating effect of the tyres, seats and suspension. The handling describes the manner in which the vehicle behaves and responds to the steering, brakes and accelerator. Roadholding describes the grip between the tyres and road surface when executing braking, accelerating and cornering manoeuvres. The roadholding and handling qualities of a vehicle can be modified by the suspension camber angles and differentials between the front and rear tyre pressures.

Due to the weight transfer generated by centrifugal force, the outer wheel on a curve exerts more cornering force than the inside tyre. This means that a vehicle with negative camber will apply an increased cornering force to the road surface. This will reduce its tendency to understeer. Conversely, a vehicle with positive camber will reduce the tendency to oversteer.

The purpose of a suspension system is to insulate the vehicle body and its occupants from road shocks, increase the tyre and road surface adhesion by maintaining contact and improve the roadholding and handling characteristics when cornering, braking and accelerating. The main types of spring used in suspension systems are coil, leaf and torsion bar. Others include various combinations of rubber, fluids and compressed gasses and air. Hydraulic dampers are used to control bounce on bumpy surfaces and anti-roll bars are fitted to reduce body roll when cornering. The effectiveness of the system is determined by the stiffness of the springs and the ratio of unsprung weight.

A vehicle with excessively hard springing will give a poor ride and the wheels will lose contact between the tyre and road surface when driven over bumps and hollows. This reduces stability and road surface adhesion. A more comfortable ride requires softer springs with plenty of suspension travel. Unfortunately however, this reduces the resistance to body roll when cornering. Excess roll means poor handling on corners and soft suspension means excessive front end dip of the front on braking and lift under acceleration.

Aerodynamic instability

Drag increases fuel consumption and holds a car back, particularly at higher speed. Modern cars are aerodynamically shaped to reduce the drag factors and improve fuel consumption. Their shape helps them slide through the air cleanly causing little air turbulence. The wedge shape of a modern car can be compared with that of an aircraft wing. The wing section is flat at the bottom to let the air travel unrestricted directly underneath. Air travelling over the top has to travel further over the curved surface making it warmer and less dense. The denser air underneath the wing pushes it up. As the air passes over a motor vehicle it creates a low pressure area over the top and produces a lift force. It is worth remembering that some four-seater aircraft have takeoff speeds of around 55 mph!

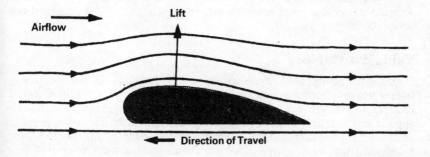

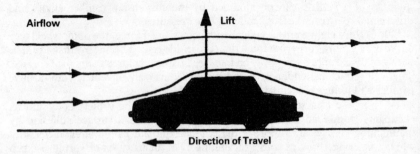

Lift forces makes a vehicle lighter and reduce the road surface adhesion, particularly at motorway speeds. Although the smoother ride and lighter steering may give an illusion of greater safety and a false sense of security, the vehicle is considerably less stable. The diagram below shows the forces acting on a vehicle when it is travelling in a straight line and under light acceleration. A motor vehicle passing through an airstream has a *centre of pressure* through which the aerodynamic forces (lift, drag and crosswind thrust) act. This can be compared with the way that weight and centrifugal force act through the *centre of gravity*. The aerodynamic stability of a vehicle is related to the relative positions of the centre of pressure and the centre of gravity. If the centre of pressure is ahead of the centre of gravity the vehicle will become unstable when driven in crosswinds.

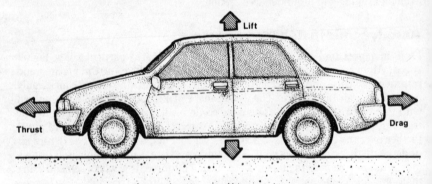

Airflow over the body of the car can also produce a significant lift force at the front of the vehicle equivalent to putting additional weight in the boot. This can result in severe oversteer or at least a reduction in the more stable understeer characteristics designed into many cars.

Vehicle instability

Inertia is the natural tendency of any mass, such as a motor car, to maintain its state of rest or uniform motion. Newton's Laws of Motion state that a moving mass will retain its velocity at a constant speed in a straight line until an external force is applied to it. Inertia will offer a resistance to the efforts of drivers to change speed or direction. The effect of inertia is readily experienced by occupants as a vehicle moves off, stops and corners. A moving vehicle is most stable when travelling straight on a level road at a constant speed. To change speed and/or direction, drivers apply an external force through tyre and road surface adhesion. These acceleration, braking and cornering forces reduce vehicle stability.

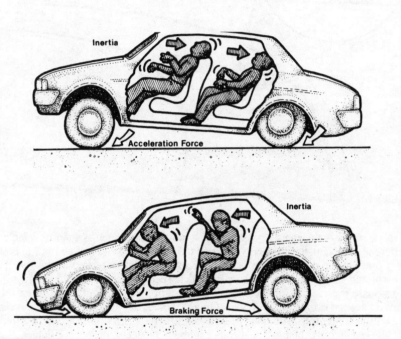

Centrifugal force is the natural reaction to and effect of centripetal force. A person standing on a bus as it swerved round a bend at high speed would say that he was flung outwards or experienced a centrifugal force. What really happened was that a centripetal force was exerted on his feet by the floor of the bus.

Centrifugal force is only an expression of the resistance offered by inertia to the centripetal (cornering) force being applied to the vehicle through the adhesion of the tyres to the road surface. The vehicle wants to go straight on and inertia will resist the centripetal (cornering) force applied at the tyres. Newton's Third Law states that the forces occur in equal and opposite pairs. Thus the cornering (centripetal) force of the tyres on the vehicle is equal and opposite to the outward thrust (centrifugal force) of the vehicle on the tyres.

Kinetic energy is the energy possessed by a moving body such as a motor vehicle. There is sufficient stored energy in a one ton vehicle travelling at 60 mph to boil two pints of ice in about four seconds. Kinetic energy is related to the vehicle weight and its speed. Any increase in vehicle speed is accompanied by a disproportionate increase in kinetic energy. For example if you double the speed the kinetic energy is four times greater. On a dry road, the braking distance of a car travelling at 40 mph, with good brakes, sound tyres and a skilled driver, is about 80 feet. At 80 mph the braking distance is about 320 feet (four times greater).

The formula is: $\frac{1}{2}MV^2$ where M = the mass and V = its velocity.

A one ton vehicle (2240 lbs) travelling at 20 mph (approx 30 ft per second) has a kinetic energy value of about 1,000,000 lbs/ft.

$$\frac{1}{2} \times 2240 = 1120 \times [(30^2) = 900] = 1,008,000 \text{ lbs/ft.}$$

At 40 mph the kinetic energy value is over 4,000,000 lbs/ft.
At 80 mph the kinetic energy value is well over 16,000,000 lbs/ft.
There is a direct relationship between these figures and those outlined in the Highway Code for braking distances. Every time the speed doubles the braking distance becomes four times greater. For example at:

20 mph the braking distance is 20 ft
40 mph the braking distance is 80 ft
80 mph the braking distance is 320 ft.

Forces applied to the car by the driver

A moving vehicle is in its most stable condition when travelling straight on a level road at a constant speed. It will remain stable until an external force is applied. Driving requires frequent changes in speed and direction. Drivers execute these changes through the application of the acceleration, braking and cornering forces. Whenever these forces are applied to the tyres, there is a natural resistance to the change they are trying to bring about which makes the vehicle less stable.

A driver's control over a motor vehicle relies totally upon the friction between the tyres and road surface. Conversely, it is the driver and the manner in which a vehicle is driven that are the most important factors affecting the level of tyre and road surface friction. To maintain friction, drivers must control the effects of inertia by cornering at appropriate speeds and by braking and accelerating smoothly and progressively. Harsh acceleration, late heavy braking and sudden changes in direction are the hallmarks of bad driving.

Acceleration force is limited by the power of an engine, the driver's skill with the accelerator, clutch and gears and the adhesion of the driving tyres to the road surface. Instability occurs when the driver applies too much force too quickly. The resistance of inertia shifts weight from the front to the rear of the vehicle and reduces the efficiency of the steering.

In extremes the natural resistance of the vehicle to accelerate may result in the driving wheels skidding on the road surface. Drivers should avoid harsh acceleration and deceleration, particularly in the lower gears and on slippery roads.

Once a cruising speed is reached, throttle openings can be reduced slightly to maintain a constant speed more economically. Remember the natural state of a moving mass is to continue travelling at a constant speed and power is needed only to overcome the effects of gravity, drag, tyre rolling resistance and friction losses in the transmission system. To reduce fuel consumption further, avoid unnecessary or fidgety movements on the accelerator pedal.

Braking force is limited by the efficiency of the brakes, the driver's skill in using them and the tyre and road surface adhesion. Engine compression provides a slight braking force when in a high gear and a significantly more pronounced effect when a low gear is engaged.

Instability occurs because the vehicle resists the applied force. The result is a shift in weight from the rear to the front of the vehicle. This makes the steering heavier to handle and reduces the adhesion of the rear tyres on the road surface.

Drivers should look well ahead for signs or obstructions and be prepared to slow down early. They should keep both hands on the wheel and try to do most of the braking whilst travelling in a straight line. An initial light braking pressure should normally be followed by a firm but progressive increase until the vehicle is pulling up short with a margin for error. This provides early warning to those behind and permits a gradual reduction in pedal pressure as the vehicle loses speed. It provides more time to assess the situation and execute gear changes. Progressive braking also maximises the comfort of passengers and their confidence in the driver. The final stage of braking is a gradual easing of the pressure to let the car roll on a little. This also reduces the risk of rear end collisions.

A common error, even in experienced drivers, is to apply the brakes either too late or too lightly in the intermediate stage. This often results in a harsh, uncontrolled last-minute application ending in frequent and unnecessary stops.

Cornering force is limited by the tyre and road surface adhesion, the efficiency of the suspension system and the driver's feel and skill with the steering wheel. Instability occurs due to the resistance of the centrifugal force to the centripetal force applied by the tyre. The result is a shift in weight to the wheels on the outside of the corner. This reduces the adhesion of the inside tyres on the road surface.

The effect of combining the cornering force with the braking and acceleration forces will cause additional imbalance to stability when the tyre adhesion and other factors may be stretched to their limit. Drivers should try to minimise the need for sudden changes in speed and direction. Braking and acceleration should be smooth and drivers should try to keep both hands on the steering wheel when the vehicle is subjected to these forces.

Try to maintain a constant speed on bends and when cornering. Try to keep two hands on the steering wheel at all times when not using other controls. Drive at lower speeds in windy weather and when contact between the tyre and the road surface is reduced in wet or icy conditions.

Drivers should slow down, or power down, before reaching bends and corners. To 'power down' means easing off the accelerator slightly. Do this whilst on the straightest course possible. The approach speed should be low enough to permit the vehicle to be driven round the bend under slight power. Except when going downhill, use a light pressure on the accelerator to maintain a constant speed. This maximises stability. Drivers should avoid sudden changes in direction and keep both hands on the wheel when cornering. Combinations of harsh acceleration or braking with cornering should also be avoided.

Drivers should slow down more than normal when approaching bends with an adverse camber as gravity will cause the vehicle to become less stable.

Factors influencing stopping distances

Stopping distances are affected by the driver's reactions, health and state of mind; the size and weight of the vehicle; the effectiveness of its braking system; the type of tyres, their pressures and depth of tread; and the condition of the road surface. Stopping distances will be greater when travelling downhill and increased considerably on wet and slippery roads.

On a dry road a car with good brakes and tyres can stop within the distances shown below, providing the driver is fit and alert. When the speed is doubled the braking distance will be quadrupled.

	Thinking distance	Braking distance		Overall stopping distance
20 mph	20 ft +	20 ft	=	40 ft
30 mph	30 ft +	45 ft	=	75 ft
40 mph	40 ft +	80 ft	=	120 ft
50 mph	50 ft +	125 ft	=	175 ft
60 mph	60 ft +	180 ft	=	240 ft
70 mph	70 ft +	245 ft	=	315 ft

The causes and correction of skidding

Although the vehicle and road surface condition may contribute to a skid, the main cause is without doubt the driver. There are three different types of skid and they are all caused either by:

- excessive speed for the road conditions and/or traffic situation
- excessive acceleration, braking and/or cornering forces applied to the tyres
- or combinations of both.

The rear wheel skid occurs when the rear wheels lose their grip. It is usually the result of excessive speeds and cornering forces. These may be in association with acceleration or more usually excessive braking force. This type of skid is easily and instantly recognised because the rear of the car slides away from the centre of the corner. Uncorrected, the vehicle may turn round completely. It is essential to eliminate the cause: release the accelerator and/or footbrake and compensate with the steering. Because the vehicle is pointing in the wrong direction, the driver's natural reaction is normally to steer back on course. There is a danger however, particularly with the quick response of radial tyres, that drivers will overreact and steer back too far.

The front wheel skid occurs when the front wheels lose their grip, leaving the driver with no directional control. It is usually the result of turning sharply into a corner or bend at excessive speed and/or under hard acceleration or braking. It is recognised because the vehicle fails to go where it is steered. Eliminate the cause and regain steering control by momentarily straightening the wheels and/or reducing pressure on the accelerator or brake.

The four wheel skid occurs when all four wheels lose their grip. It is usually due to travelling at excessive speeds for the road conditions or traffic situation, resulting in uncontrolled overbraking. On a wet or slippery surface drivers may even feel they are increasing speed. It leaves them with no control over direction and may result in a combination of turning broadside with no response to steering corrections. Steering control can be partially restored by momentarily releasing the brake to allow wheel rotation to recover and then quickly re-applying it in a rapid on-off action.

The prevention of skids is better than the cure!

It is important to recognise danger signs and act on them. For example, slowing down early upon sighting a group of children playing near the road will subsequently mean less braking pressure is needed if one of them dashes out. Concentration, planning and the early anticipation of the possible actions of others is essential. In snow and ice slow down early with light braking pressure. Gentle braking is less likely to cause skidding than changing into a lower gear. Use gradual acceleration and keep in the highest gear possible without distressing the engine. When going uphill in snow try to maintain a steady momentum by staying well back from the vehicle ahead.

Drive at safe speeds for the road surface conditions. Accelerate, brake and corner gently. Drive slower on wet, icy and slippery surfaces. Watch out for loose gravel, fallen leaves and damp patches under trees. Make sure your tyres are correctly inflated and that they have a minimum of 2 mm of tread all around. Never mix crossply and radial tyres on the same axle.

Keep off soft verges! Read the surface conditions and slow down well before reaching any bumpy parts of the road or where the edges are rough and broken. Avoid heavy braking on loose gravel, muddy surfaces and on damp patches under trees. The combination of oil, rubber dust and water can make the surface very slippery after a light summer shower following a long dry spell. In freezing temperatures remember that black ice forms on exposed bridges first.

Emergency braking

Drivers should be realistic about the distance it takes to stop, particularly in wet conditions. Pivot promptly to the brake and apply it progressively and firmly. Keep both hands on the wheel and try to keep the vehicle on a straight course. Maximum braking force is applied to the vehicle just before the wheels lock. It is most important to avoid braking so hard that the wheels lock as this will considerably lengthen the stopping distance. Pushing the clutch down too soon will increase the risk of locking the wheels and lengthen the stopping distance.

Particularly in wet, slippery conditions, where the driver has applied too much pressure and locked the wheels, the brake should be momentarily released to allow the tyres to regain their grip, and quickly re-applied. This method of rapid on-off braking can be likened to the very rapid on-off action of automatic braking systems. It gives the driver greater braking efficiency and increased directional control in emergency situations where the natural reaction is to lock the wheels.

Cadence braking

This specialised technique relies, in part, on the fact that the front brakes provide more stopping power than the rear. As the brakes are applied, weight transfers from the rear of the vehicle and some forward momentum is absorbed by the compression of the front springs. This extra weight on the front tyres reduces the risk of 'locking up'. Braking is carried out in rhythm with compression and decompression of the front and rear suspensions. The technique is used in high performance track and rally driving and is unsuited for on-road use. It involves applying the brakes hard to compress the front suspension. As the suspension dips the brakes are momentarily released to allow the suspension to rise. As the suspension dips again at the top of the rise, the brakes are re-applied and so on.

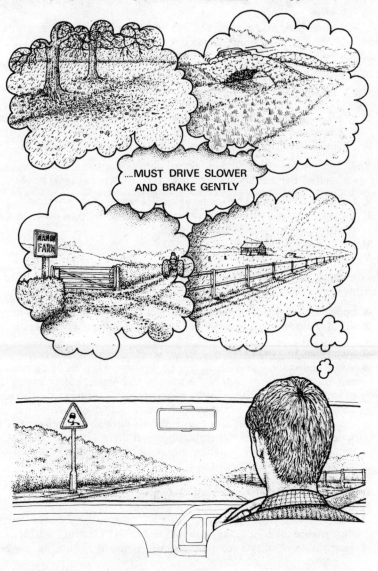

Systems of car control

The natural phenomena and forces that affect the stability of a vehicle in motion are scientific facts of which any system of car control must take proper account. An efficient system will help to give drivers sufficient time to see and assess correctly the road and traffic conditions. It will have a built-in set of safety margins which help them to compensate for inevitable errors, mistakes made by other road users and minor lapses in concentration. An efficient system will ensure drivers have time to control their vehicle in a proper and sympathetic manner.

Drivers should try to incorporate the following tried and tested principles into their system of car control.

Vehicle speed should never exceed that which permits the driver to bring the vehicle to a properly controlled stop well within the distance that can be seen to be clear. Drivers should look for and respond to:

- actual obstructions to the intended course
- the potential of other road users to move out of blind areas behind obstructions into or across the intended course
- restrictions to the driver's sightlines caused by road features such as bends, hillcrests and hollows (dead ground)
- potential obstructions which may be hidden by restricted sightlines.

Vehicle control and speed should take account of the natural phenomena and forces that affect the stability of a vehicle in motion. Drivers should be aware of:

- the physical roadholding and handling limitations of their vehicle
- the tyre and road surface adhesion and increased stopping distances resulting from wet and icy conditions
- the effects of camber and gravity on hills
- aerodynamic forces acting on the vehicle.

To minimise the effects of the natural phenomena and forces that affect the stability of a vehicle in motion, drivers should:

- apply and remove acceleration, braking and cornering forces smoothly
- avoid excessive acceleration and/or braking forces when negotiating a curved path
- avoid changing gear when negotiating severe changes in direction
- avoid unnecessary gear changing. Be selective when changing down, for example: keep both hands on the wheel whilst braking; after slowing down to less than 10 mph and as the breaking pressure is being gradually reduced and/or released, change direct from fourth gear to second. Gears enable drivers to maintain efficient engine speeds through a wide range of road speeds and different power requirements. Although in some circumstances gears can legitimately be used as a braking source, generally it is no longer considered good driving practice
- keep both hands on the steering wheel when braking and cornering
- keep both hands on the steering wheel when accelerating hard
- use gentle controlled power when negotiating a curved path
- when stationary for more than the time it takes to comfortably apply and then release the handbrake, it should be applied, even on a level road. For example a one to two second pause will normally involve the use of the

handbrake. Having said this, it should also be stated that experienced drivers rarely come to complete stops for this length of time. By planning their approach to situations likely to require stops, they are creeping at very low speeds on the final two or three yards before the stop is required. This often gives the situation time to clear, enabling them to move off again before stopping completely. In such circumstances using the handbrake is inappropriate.

Drivers who are sympathetic to the needs of their vehicle not only prolong its working life but make more efficient use of fuel. Drivers should:

- avoid unnecessary or fidgety movements on the accelerator
- use the accelerator and/or footbrake early and smoothly
- avoid excessive clutch slip, drag and unnecessary coasting
- avoid excessive tyre wear by cornering at lower speeds
- avoid using gears unnecessarily to reduce speed
- switch off the engine whilst stationary for prolonged periods
- avoid switching the car's interior heating system on before the engine is hot
- avoid additional drag caused by roof racks
- avoid unnecessary loads in the boot
- keep engines properly tuned
- check tyres regularly for uneven wear and pressure
- have brakes and vehicle serviced regularly
- keep a regular eye on the bodywork for corrosion.

Gear-assisted braking

Changing down to reduce speed is unsympathetic to the vehicle, wastes petrol and is not normally acceptable as good driving practice. However, a lower gear can be engaged to offset the effects of gravity on downhill gradients. The brakes should be used first, however, to bring the speed under control before selecting an appropriate lower gear. This provides increased engine braking and reduces the risk of brake failure from overheating due to continuous use down long hills.

Selective gear changing

To slow down: keep two hands on the wheel, use the footbrake to reduce speed and after slowing down change down, if necessary, before reaching the hazard.

Approaching a simple left turn in fourth gear, use the brake to slow down to less than 10 mph and change directly to second as you are easing the pressure from the brake or after it is fully released.

Approaching the end of a road in third or fourth gear where visibility is restricted, use the brake to slow down until you have almost stopped. Push the clutch down and gradually ease the braking pressure to let the vehicle roll. Just before it stops, change into first gear ready for moving away.

The power change

This technique permits lower gears to be selected smoothly when travelling at higher than normal speeds. It matches the engine speed to the lower gear and enables them to be engaged quickly without the loss of road speed or power. It is beneficial where extra power is needed for overtaking or climbing a hill.

To change: hand on the gear lever and cover the clutch, clutch down quickly and depress the accelerator, release it immediately and select the lower gear, raise the clutch and accelerate as appropriate.

Double de-clutch

This specialised gear changing technique is generally only necessary in some heavy goods vehicles. Although it is still recommended in some advanced driving manuals, it is inappropriate in modern vehicles with synchromesh gears and may increase wear and tear.

To change up: hand on gear lever and cover the clutch, clutch down and off the accelerator, move the gear lever to neutral, clutch up quickly and then down again, engage the higher gear, finally raise the clutch and accelerate.

To change down: hand on gear lever and cover the clutch, clutch down and off the accelerator, move the gear lever to neutral, clutch up and depress the accelerator quickly – releasing it immediately; clutch down quickly and engage the lower gear, finally raise the clutch and continue braking/accelerating.

Heel and toe

This specialised technique is used in high performance driving and is unsuited for normal on-road use. It permits the driver to make a power change into a lower gear by blipping the accelerator with the heel or side of the right foot whilst braking with the ball of the foot.

Anticipate the effects of strong side winds

Expect strong side winds in high exposed places. Hold the wheel firmly and be ready to compensate for any deflection when passing high-sided vehicles or after passing through bridges. Remember, others at your sides may also be affected.

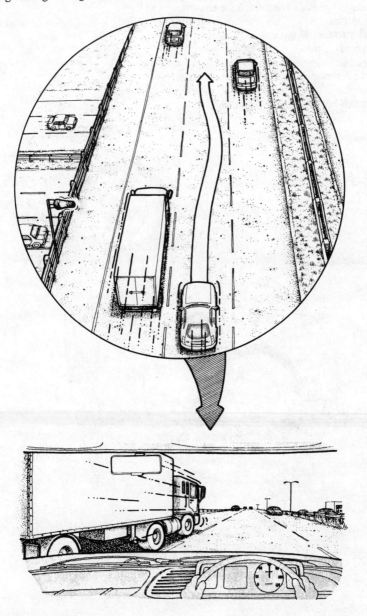

How to avoid aquaplaning

Replace worn tyres and drive more slowly on wet surfaces. A cushion of undisplaced water builds up just ahead of the tyres. At higher speeds the tyres ride up onto the cushion and lose contact with the road surface. If aquaplaning occurs the driver has no control over speed or direction.

With new tyres it can occur at less than 60 mph. With worn tyres it will happen at much lower speeds.

3 Advanced Driving Skills

The system of car control

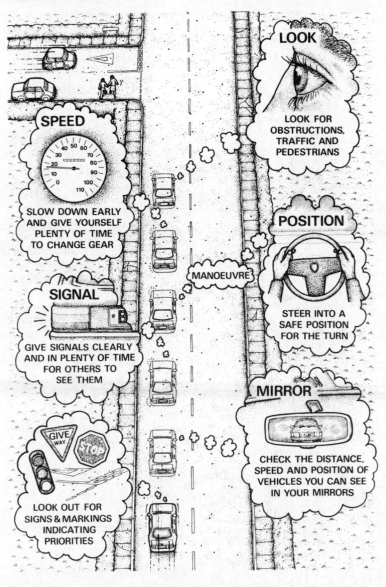

Avoid accidents caused by incorrect positioning

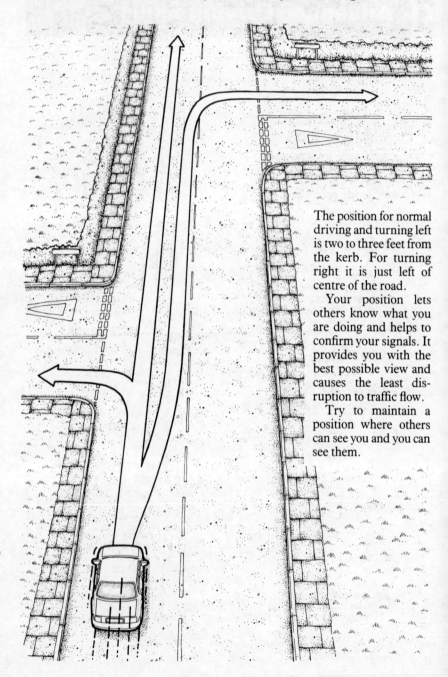

The position for normal driving and turning left is two to three feet from the kerb. For turning right it is just left of centre of the road.

Your position lets others know what you are doing and helps to confirm your signals. It provides you with the best possible view and causes the least disruption to traffic flow.

Try to maintain a position where others can see you and you can see them.

Cross the path of oncoming traffic safely

You must give way to closely approaching oncoming traffic. Try to time your arrival at the point of turn to coincide with their passing the junction.

If you are unable to do this and reach the point of turn first, stop and wait just short of it.

Point of Turn

When turning near bends and hillcrests your view may be restricted. Beware of vehicles approaching just out of sight.

Look into the side road before turning

Avoid cutting corners

As you move up to the point of turn be sure to look into the new road.

Watch out for parked cars and road works and wait for any pedestrians crossing.

Give way to pedestrians crossing the road into which you are turning

Be prepared to wait for pedestrians crossing the side road. Watch out, particularly for those walking with their back to you. In some instances it may be appropriate to sound the horn lightly.

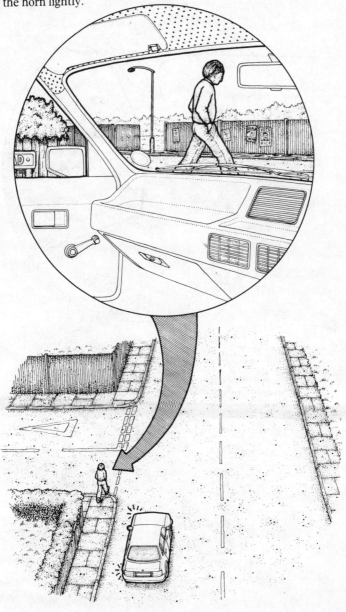

Give way to pedestrians crossing as you approach the end of a road

Look out for pedestrians and hold back when they are crossing the road. Approach busy shopping streets very slowly.

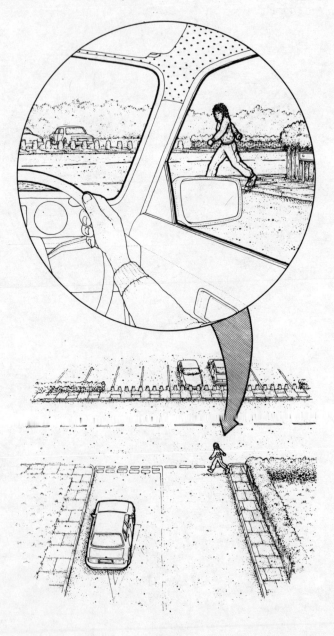

Leave drivers of large vehicles room to manoeuvre

When large vehicles are turning, hold well back and allow plenty of space for them to cut, or swing wide on, the corner.

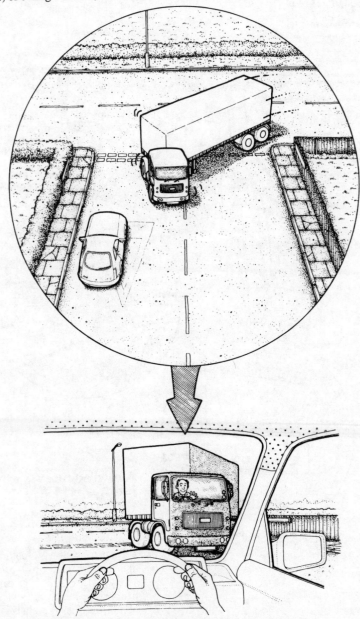

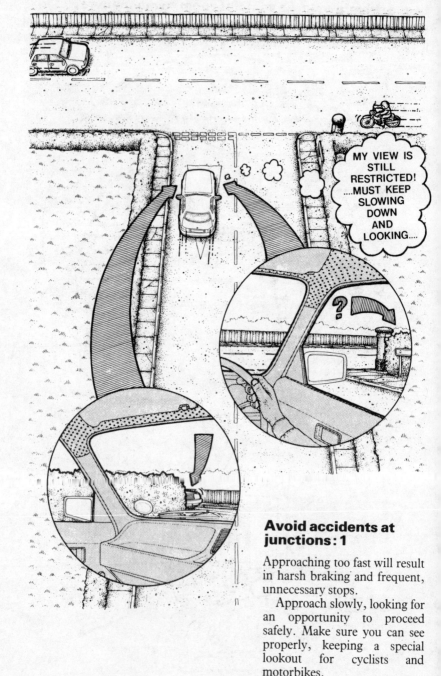

MY VIEW IS STILL RESTRICTED! ....MUST KEEP SLOWING DOWN AND LOOKING....

Avoid accidents at junctions: 1

Approaching too fast will result in harsh braking and frequent, unnecessary stops.

Approach slowly, looking for an opportunity to proceed safely. Make sure you can see properly, keeping a special lookout for cyclists and motorbikes.

Avoid accidents at junctions: 2

Vehicles parked near junctions will seriously restrict your view of traffic travelling along the main road.

Creep slowly forwards, looking both ways for approaching vehicles hidden behind obstructions.

Make sure you can see properly before deciding to proceed and watch for vehicles approaching from your left.

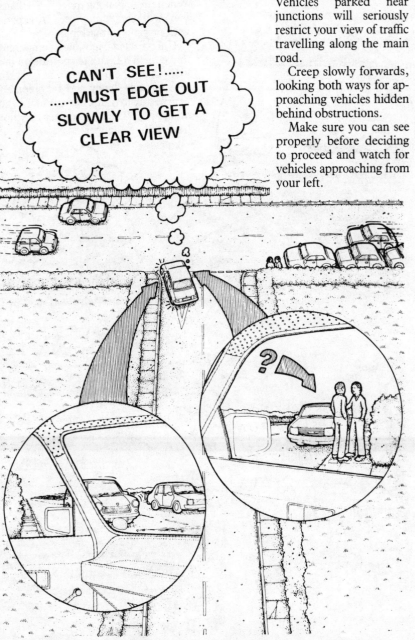

Avoiding accidents at minor crossroads

When driving along quiet side streets you will sometimes see crossroads with no signs or markings.

Unrestricted sightlines sometimes make them difficult to spot. Be on the lookout for them.

Approach slowly and be prepared to give way to traffic moving along the other road. The other driver may not have seen the danger!

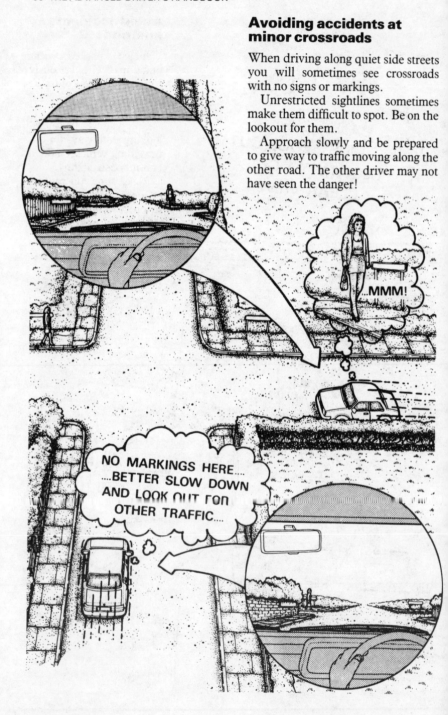

Avoiding accidents when driving in lanes

You should normally keep to the left lane unless turning right or overtaking. Drive in the middle of your lane and look and plan well ahead to make sure you don't get boxed in behind parked vehicles. When you see others wanting to move out into the lane ahead of you, hold back and let them.

On one-way streets expect traffic passing you on either side and remember that pedestrians are sometimes disoriented about which way to look for traffic. Watch out for them stepping into the road, especially if you are driving along in the right-hand lane.

Avoiding accidents at major crossroads

When driving straight ahead at a busy junction you should normally approach in the left lane. This reduces the risk of other vehicles passing on your left and avoids unnecessary lane changes to regain the normal driving position at the other side of the junction.

Where there are two or more lanes marked with arrows pointing straight on, think ahead and choose the most convenient one. To do this look ahead for obstructions and use your knowledge of the area.

To turn right from a busy multi-laned road, you should normally approach in the right-hand lane. Get into position early and without disrupting other traffic. To do this, try to maintain your speed while you check your mirrors for traffic coming up behind and at your sides. Reducing speed may encourage following traffic to overtake and prevent you from changing lanes in time. Be prepared to increase speed if necessary to move safely over or hold back and wait for a larger space in the traffic. Think ahead and try not to get boxed in. *Do not change lanes suddenly!*

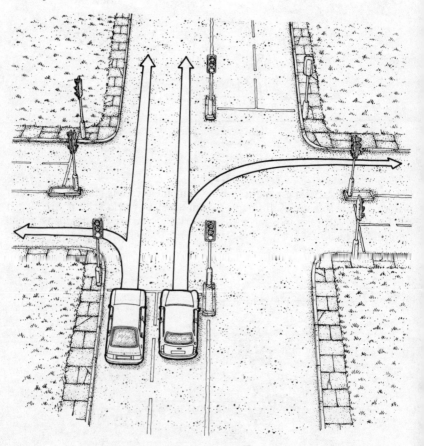

Choosing the most appropriate lane : 1

Avoid straddling lanes, particularly when approaching junctions or passing stationary vehicles. Where there are parked vehicles or other obstructions blocking the left lane at the far side, the junction should normally be negotiated in the right-hand lane. Watch out for right-turning vehicles ahead though! These are sometimes delayed for long periods whilst they wait for oncoming traffic. If you have to wait behind them you may be delayed for a long time.

Where you see right-turning traffic it is normally better to choose the left lane, even if you see there is an obstruction at the other side of the junction.

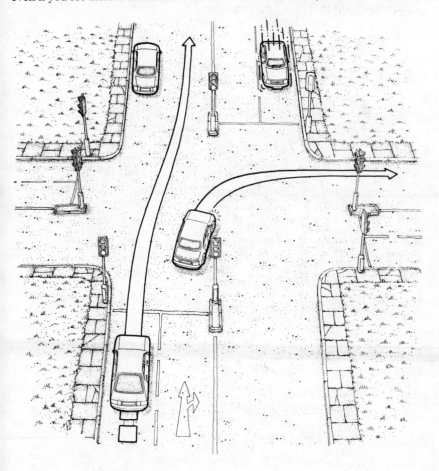

Choosing the most appropriate lane: 2

At some junctions the road markings and normal rules for positioning vary. Watch out for them and get into position as early as you can. At junctions with two or more lanes marked with arrows pointing in the direction you wish to take, choose the most convenient one. To do this, use your knowledge of the area or try to work out where you are going at the next junction and which lane you will need when you get there.

After selecting a lane, drive in the middle of it and stay there throughout the turn. Unless you need the right lane at the next junction you should normally return to the left after completing the turn.

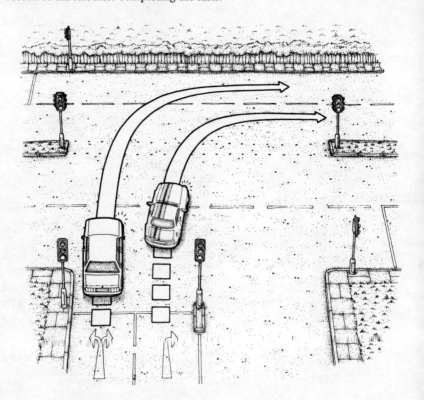

Be prepared to give way and wait for oncoming traffic

The right turn at traffic lights is one of the most dangerous manoeuvres!

Before turning, be prepared to give way to oncoming vehicles. Wait just short of the point of turn for a suitable break in the traffic. If it is very busy, you may have to wait until the lights change. When this happens you should normally clear the junction as quickly as you can but be sure the oncoming traffic is stopping.

If there is a right filter arrow, you may turn that way regardless of any other lights showing. What if oncoming vehicles continue to come through the junction? Make sure they are stopping before you turn!

Because you proceeded to turn through a green light, is no consolation to you, your family or your company, if you have to spend the rest of your life in a wheelchair.

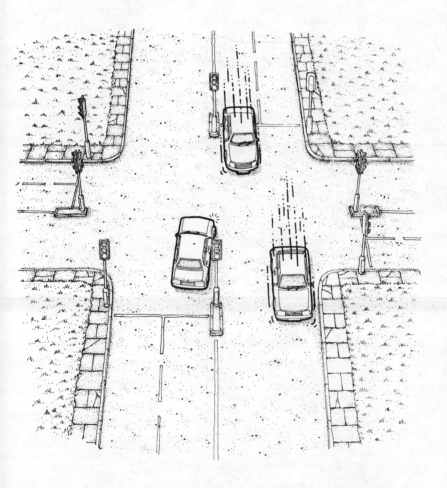

Negotiating offside-to-offside turns safely

When second in line to turn right, hold back or the road will become blocked. Those first in line should move slowly forwards to the point of turn and drive around the rear of the other vehicle. *Look and be prepared to wait for any oncoming vehicles* travelling through the junction in the far lane.

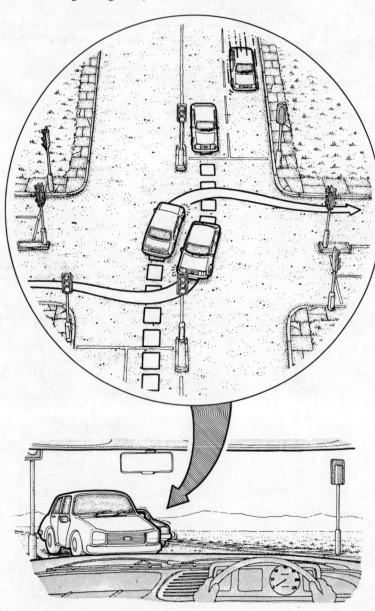

Negotiating nearside-to-nearside turns safely

Due to the size or position of other vehicles, and the junction layout or markings, this method of turning right is sometimes more appropriate. It enables more vehicles to turn in less time. Watch the actions and position of the oncoming vehicles. Move slowly forwards steering slightly to the right. *Look and be prepared to wait for oncoming traffic.*

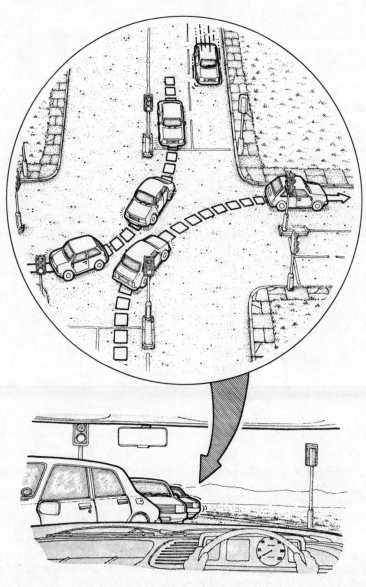

Avoiding accidents when negotiating roundabouts: 1

Long before you reach a roundabout, look for, and make a mental note of, the position of your exit road. Take short, frequent looks as you approach. Let traffic coming from your right go first but, if you can, try to time your arrival to coincide with a gap in the traffic.

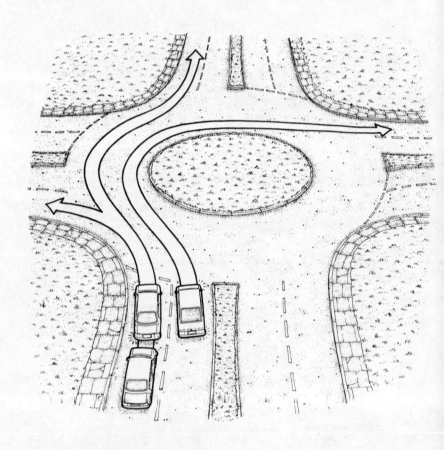

When turning left, signal and approach in the left lane. Keep the signal on and maintain the left lane on the roundabout and into the exit road.

When following the road ahead, you should normally approach in the left lane and stay in it. As you pass the exit just before yours, give a left signal for leaving the roundabout by the next one.

When turning right, signal and approach in the right lane. Keep the signal on and stay in the right lane as you drive round the roundabout. As you approach the exit just before yours, check for vehicles in the nearside lane and change the signal to left. You should normally leave in the left lane if it is clear.

Avoiding accidents when negotiating roundabouts: 2

Look well ahead for road markings giving directions which vary from the basic rules. Get into position early and stay in the middle of the lane selected.

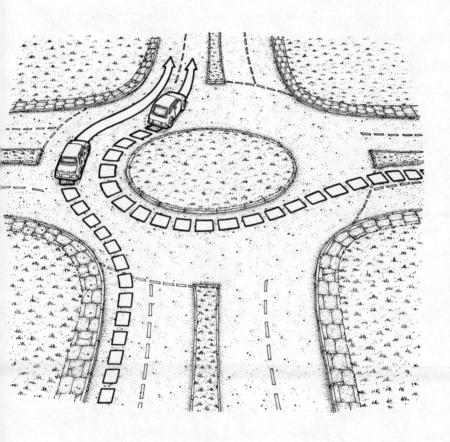

Build up and maintain a reasonable speed on the roundabout. Crawling round may result in other drivers passing on your nearside as you are trying to leave. Always check for vehicles passing on your left side before leaving a roundabout. Where vehicles are coming through on the nearside, or the exit lane is blocked, leave the roundabout in the right-hand lane.

Plan for the next turn and choose the most appropriate lane

Plan well ahead to avoid last-minute lane changes over short distances. Use your knowledge of the area, or try to work out where you are going and which lane you will need at the next junction. For example, the lane you need for the approach to the second of these two roundabouts should influence your choice at the first.

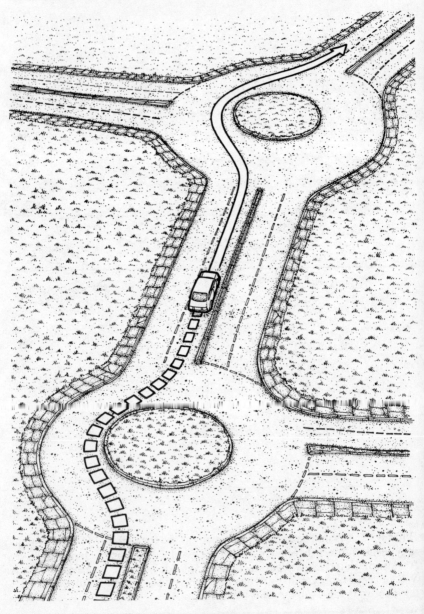

Driving in queues of slow-moving traffic

Circumstances may put you in the wrong lane! Where you are unable to change safely, be prepared to stay in it and miss your turning. In a queue of very slow-moving or stationary traffic it may be possible to change lanes safely with a combination of signals and eye contact followed by a gradual change in position. Put your signal on and then look at the driver just to your rear. If you can make eye contact and smile they are almost sure to let you in. The secret of carrying out this manoeuvre safely is to drive slowly, change direction gradually but positively. Avoid sudden changes in direction or spurts of speed and watch out for motor-cyclists and cyclists riding between the lanes.

Consideration and eye contact

Stop short of junctions when waiting in lines of traffic. This allows oncoming vehicles to turn right into side roads.

Next time you're waiting to move out of a side road in these conditions, or when the other traffic is moving very slowly, look at the passing drivers and make eye contact. If you can attract their attention, they are almost certain to hold back and let you out.

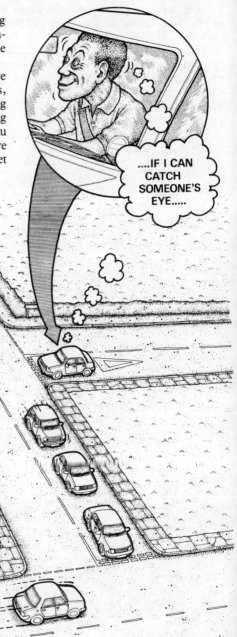

4 Defensive Driving Techniques

What is defensive driving?

Defensive driving involves the ability to plan well ahead, predict the actions of other people and compensate for their mistakes. It places most emphasis on the development of hazard awareness, self-control and other important skills used to avoid accidents.

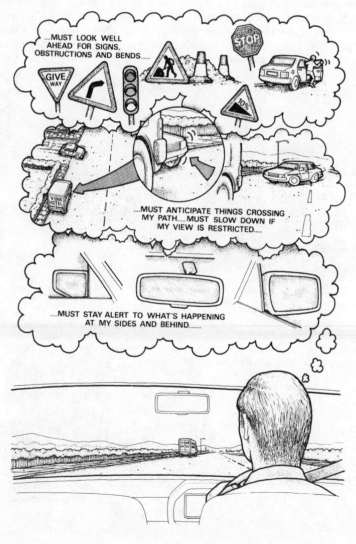

Plan ahead and work things out in advance

Approaching red traffic lights be prepared to slow down early. This gives more time for them to change. Only proceed through a green light when you are sure it is safe to do so and your intended exit is clear. If not, wait until you can move across the junction without blocking it. Approaching a green light, look and be prepared to hold back for: vehicles moving along the other road; oncoming drivers turning across your path; and pedestrians crossing the road.

Remember that all colours except green mean stop. Try to predict when the lights may change and be ready to pull up. At some point on the approach, however, you will find yourself too close to stop safely. Once past this point you should normally continue.

Work things out as you approach, check how close following vehicles are and how fast they are travelling. Continually re-assess what you will do if the lights change. This saves critical split seconds if amber appears, by enabling you to make an instant decision to go on or pull up.

Awareness to the rear: 1

Use the mirrors frequently as you drive along. With practice, peripheral vision can detect movement in the mirrors and attract your attention to them at critical times provided they are adjusted perfectly to the natural driving position of your eyes.

As an experienced driver, you should be conscious of the traffic situation behind at any time and able to judge the speeds and distances involved. Take particular note of vehicles moving into the blind areas at your sides.

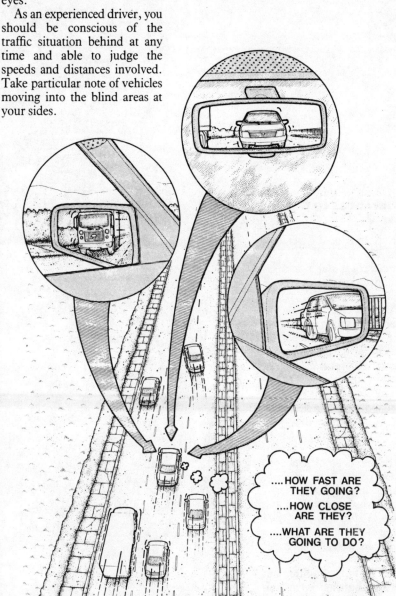

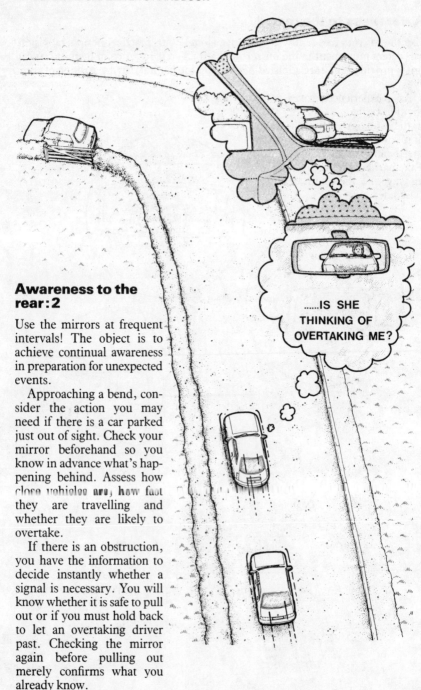

......IS SHE
THINKING OF
OVERTAKING ME?

Awareness to the rear: 2

Use the mirrors at frequent intervals! The object is to achieve continual awareness in preparation for unexpected events.

Approaching a bend, consider the action you may need if there is a car parked just out of sight. Check your mirror beforehand so you know in advance what's happening behind. Assess how close vehicles are, how fast they are travelling and whether they are likely to overtake.

If there is an obstruction, you have the information to decide instantly whether a signal is necessary. You will know whether it is safe to pull out or if you must hold back to let an overtaking driver past. Checking the mirror again before pulling out merely confirms what you already know.

Position approaching right and left bends

Approach right-hand bends in the normal driving position close to the left kerb. This increases your view into the bend. Obvious consideration should be given to nearside dangers which require a greater margin of safety, adverse cambers or the poor condition of the road edge.

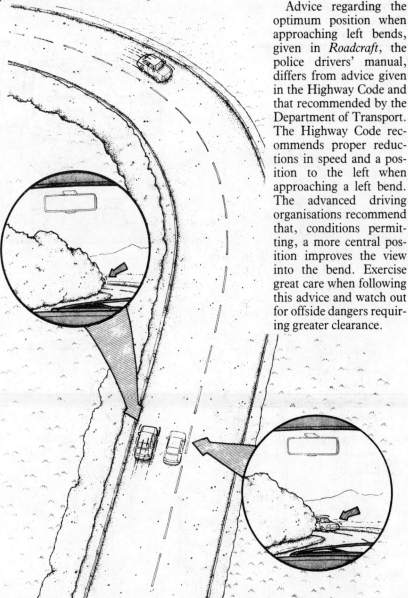

Advice regarding the optimum position when approaching left bends, given in *Roadcraft*, the police drivers' manual, differs from advice given in the Highway Code and that recommended by the Department of Transport. The Highway Code recommends proper reductions in speed and a position to the left when approaching a left bend. The advanced driving organisations recommend that, conditions permitting, a more central position improves the view into the bend. Exercise great care when following this advice and watch out for offside dangers requiring greater clearance.

Avoid accidents with overtaking vehicles

As you drive along watch out for overtaking vehicles and leave them room to get back in. Use your side mirrors again before turning, changing lanes and leaving roundabouts.

After signalling to turn, allow time for drivers behind to see it. Check they are responding correctly and decide if your intended manoeuvre can be carried out safely.

Be prepared to let them go!

Using the mirror to avoid accidents with cyclists and motorcyclists

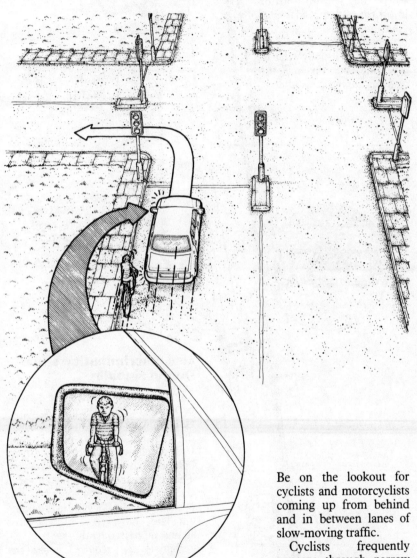

Be on the lookout for cyclists and motorcyclists coming up from behind and in between lanes of slow-moving traffic.

Cyclists frequently squeeze through narrow gaps. After waiting to turn left, check the nearside door mirror or blind spot before moving off.

Do you need to signal?

Signals should be given where they help to warn or inform any other road user of your intentions. If you are unsure whether a signal is needed, it is usually safer to give one, but this *will not make an unsafe action safe.*

DOES HE REALISE I'LL BE PULLING OUT?

.....WILL A SIGNAL HELP?.....

Use discrimination when giving signals

Signals used too often for passing parked cars can reduce their impact and following drivers may then ignore those given later for turning right. Unless following too closely, drivers behind can normally see ahead of you. They can usually tell from your speed and position that you intend to pass parked vehicles. If you leave pulling out late, however, you will need signals more frequently.

Signals are required more frequently for pulling out to pass obstructions when following traffic is coming up fast or is already in a lane to your right, or when driving in fog or poor light conditions.

Signals that need special timing

Some signals need to be delayed; for example, if you want to turn left and have yet to pull out to pass a parked vehicle.

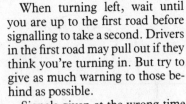

When turning left, wait until you are up to the first road before signalling to take a second. Drivers in the first road may pull out if they think you're turning in. But try to give as much warning to those behind as possible.

Signals given at the wrong time may panic others into taking unnecessary evasive action. Before giving any signal you should consider its effect on them. For example, delay the right turn signal for changing lanes where drivers behind are in the act of overtaking.

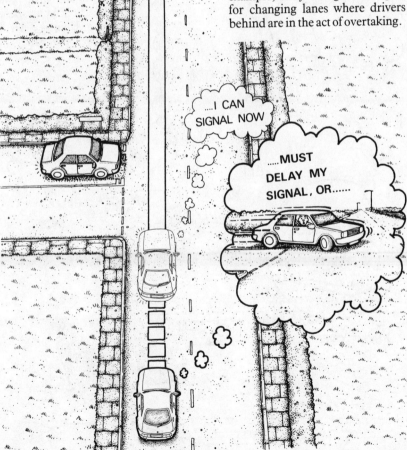

Avoiding motorway accidents

Drive in the left lane and keep at least two seconds back from the vehicle ahead. The middle and right-hand lanes are only for overtaking.

Use the mirrors frequently and avoid changing lanes unnecessarily.

Allow others to move into the lane ahead of you from slip roads and where motorways merge.

When leaving the motorway, get into the left lane early. After periods of sustained high speed you may find you are going faster than you think. Check your speed before reaching the end of the deceleration lane.

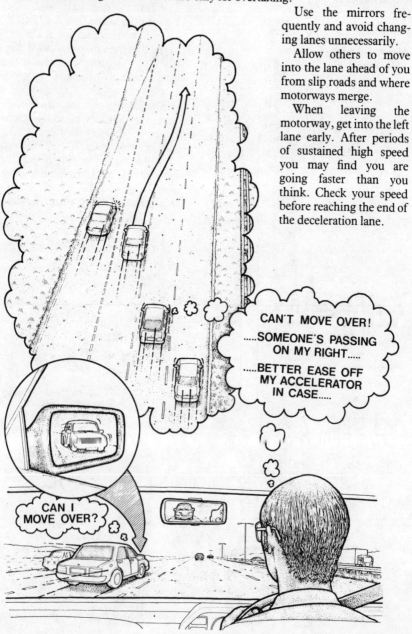

Avoiding motorway disasters

It is not speed that kills but lack of thought, restraint and skill on the part of drivers using motorways. Motorways carry more traffic for greater distances at higher speeds. Despite this they are still our safest roads: that is, until something goes wrong. To avoid motorway disasters the important rules are to:

- keep back from the vehicle ahead
- use the mirrors well before changing lanes (and remember the blind spots)
- stay alert and concentrate on what is happening ahead
- drive slower in poor conditions and observe speed limit signs.

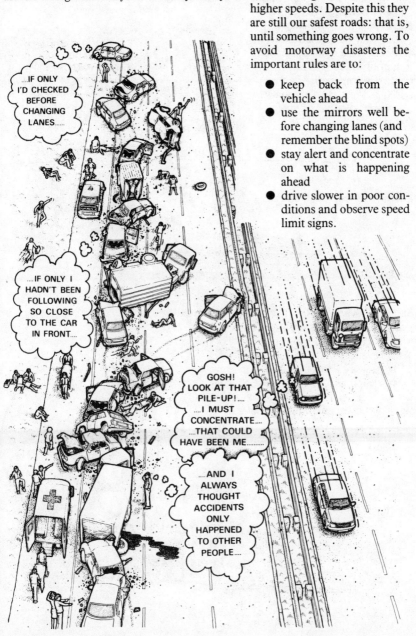

Can you stop within the distance you can see to be clear?

Advanced drivers leave margins for error and keep to speeds at which they can pull up comfortably well within the distance they can see to be clear.

Take nothing for granted and expect things to change!

Look for people and other vehicles and predict the potential for movement into or across your path. Be prepared to take precautionary measures such as reducing speed.

Stationary vehicles restrict your view of people crossing the road and drivers who may be emerging from junctions. They also prevent them from seeing you.

Be prepared to slow down and allow extra clearance. As you approach, look through car windows and underneath for signs of movement or other danger.

Avoid accidents near bends and hillcrests

Are you prepared for vehicles just out of sight, turning across your path or pedestrians crossing the road just round the bend? Be ready to slow down!

Expect oncoming traffic passing parked vehicles driving along your side of the road. Be ready to hold back and allow time for other drivers to return to their own side.

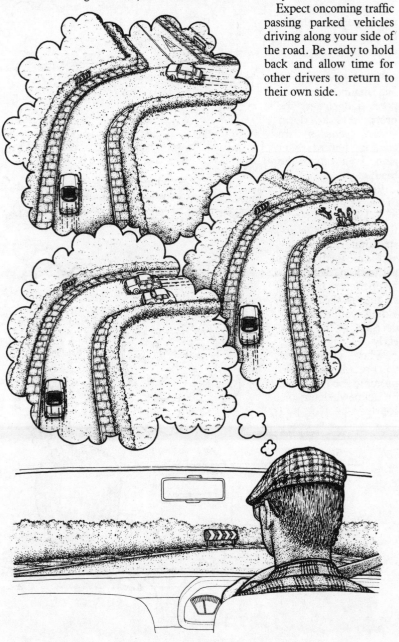

Avoid accidents with oncoming vehicles

It can be dangerous to assume that oncoming drivers will give way where parked vehicles or other obstructions are on their side of the road.

Whether caused by bad manners, or just poor judgement, be prepared to slow down where vehicles are coming towards you along your side of the road.

Judge the speed and distances involved and how long it will take them to reach the obstruction. Hold back and leave them time to get back in. Minor adjustments are normally all that is needed providing you make the decision to hold back early.

When others give you precedence, help to promote good manners by acknowledging the courtesy.

.....I'M GLAD I SLOWED DOWN TO LET HIM THROUGH!

Avoid accidents with right turning vehicles

What if . . . an oncoming driver turns across your path? It is dangerous to assume others will give way to you when they turn right. Be prepared!

This often occurs at traffic lights, particularly if your car is masked by stationary or slower moving vehicles in the lane to your right!

Be wary of oncoming vehicles where the driver is signalling to turn right. Be prepared to hold back if you think they may turn across your path.

Remember, as long as you make your decision to hold back early, minor speed adjustments are all that will normally be needed.

Judge the speed, distance and time it will take them to reach the point of turn. Look at the driver, try to make eye contact and be on your guard.

It is no consolation to your family, that the accident which put you in hospital was someone else's fault!

Make sure others can see you!

Use dipped headlights to ensure other road users can see you clearly at night and in poor daylight conditions such as fog, heavy rain and falling snow.

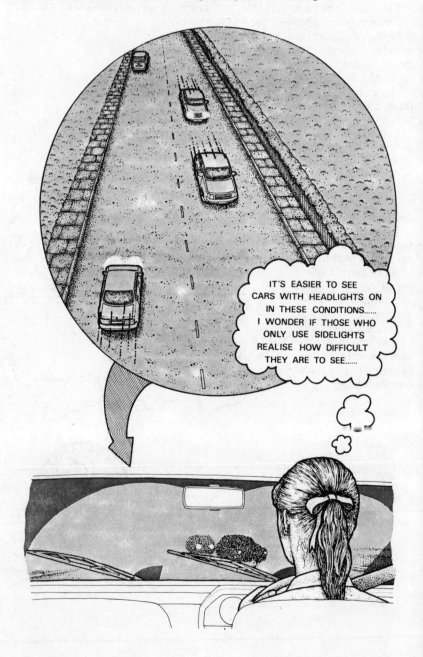

How to avoid accidents when driving in the dark

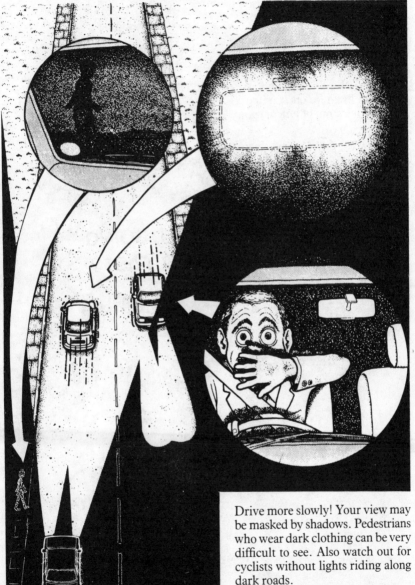

Drive more slowly! Your view may be masked by shadows. Pedestrians who wear dark clothing can be very difficult to see. Also watch out for cyclists without lights riding along dark roads.

Dip your headlights! Don't dazzle the drivers of oncoming vehicles, nor those driving ahead of you.

How to avoid accidents when driving in fog

Avoid parking on the road in fog!

Keep windows free of condensation and watch out for obstructions in the road. Other drivers may not have their headlights on so use your ears as well as your eyes. Wind your window down and listen for other traffic before moving out of junctions.

Avoiding accidents with vehicles ahead: 1

One yard for each mph of speed is normally considered to be a safe, two-second, following distance.

Stay further back from large and slow moving vehicles. This improves your view and gives you more time to respond if the driver stops.

Don't let drivers following behind too closely cause you to drive faster than you feel is safe. Drop further back from the vehicle ahead. This gives you some breathing space and allows extra time to brake gently and gives drivers behind more time to pull up.

Avoiding accidents with vehicles ahead : 2

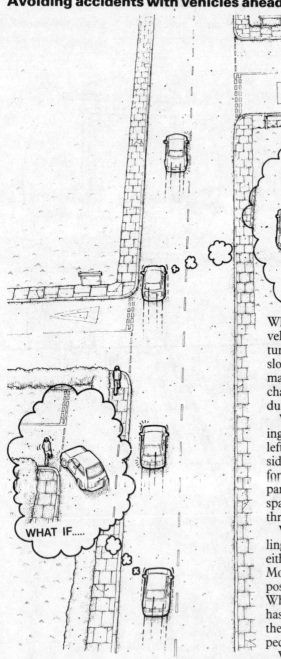

SLOW DOWN
IN CASE......

WHAT IF.....

Where the driver of the vehicle ahead is signalling to turn, they are almost sure to slow down to execute the manoeuvre. Anticipate any change in position and reduction in speed.

Where the vehicle is turning right, position well to the left ready to pass on its nearside. If the driver has to wait for oncoming traffic, be prepared to hold back if the space is too small to get through safely.

Where the driver is signalling left, the vehicle may either be stopping or turning. Move into an overtaking position but hold well back. What if . . . the driver in front has to stop and wait because the side road is blocked or pedestrians are crossing?

What if . . . drivers waiting in the side road pull out?

Avoiding accidents with vehicles ahead:3

When driving at higher speeds look well ahead for obstructions in your lane. Look for vehicles slowing down to turn or those waiting in the central reserve.

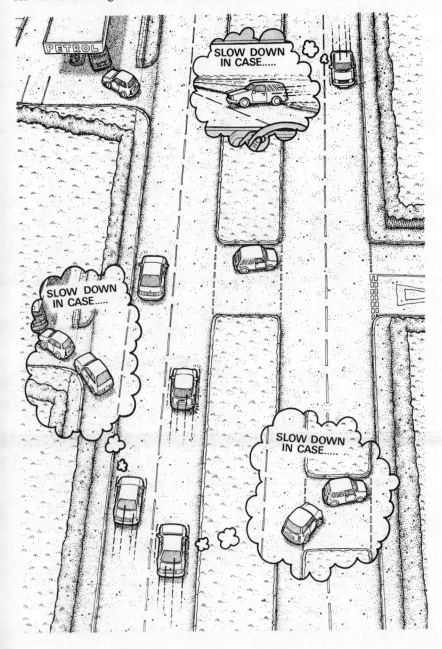

Give way to oncoming traffic

Where there are obstructions on your side, be prepared to hold back and give way to oncoming traffic. Position towards the centre to give a better view and reduce the risk of being boxed in.

Hold back until you can leave four or five feet clearance. In busy conditions, it may be necessary to feel your way through narrower gaps. Consider the speed of oncoming vehicles and adjust your own accordingly.

Avoiding accidents near buses and stationary vehicles

What if . . . the bus driver pulls up? Many do with little or no warning! Stay well back and watch out for signals or other signs that they may be stopping: for example, where you can see people queueing at a stop or standing at the door of the bus to get off. Follow in an overtaking position which gives a clear view ahead and hold back until a safe opportunity arises to get by.

Expect bus drivers to signal and move straight out from bus stops as you are approaching or passing. Be prepared to hold back and let them go!

Leaving extra clearance provides a better view into the blind area behind the obstruction. Watch out for people stepping out from behind buses, or any other stationary vehicle, or running across from the other side of the road to catch them!

Avoiding accidents with cyclists: 1

Stay well back until you can leave five or six feet clearance without endangering oncoming drivers. Follow in this position to give the cyclist confidence, to make passing easier and prevent following drivers boxing you in.

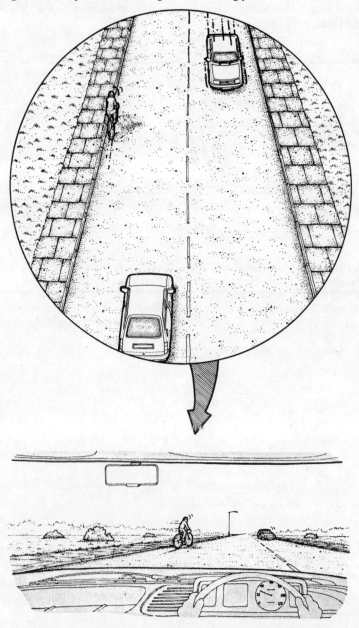

Avoiding accidents with cyclists : 2

Leave cyclists plenty of clearance. The closer you get the more they will wobble! When unable to pass them, slow down, keep in an overtaking position but stay well back until you are sure you can get by safely.

What if . . . their steering becomes erratic when they are struggling to pedal uphill or if they swerve to avoid roadside grates and potholes?

What if . . . you fail to see them because they are riding along close to the kerb as you emerge from road junctions? Think once, thick twice – think *bike!*

What if . . . they have no lights on at night? In poor weather conditions and when wearing dark clothing they are also difficult to see.

No-one wants a child's life on their conscience! Hold back if you sense something is wrong.

Be patient and allow even more space. Youngsters don't always understand Highway Code rules or the significance of position and the meaning of their signals.

They may occasionally signal one way and turn the other.

What if . . . they ride along on the wrong side of the road towards you or pull straight out of the junction without looking?

Watch out for 'Look, no hands!' displays and unusual actions like 'wheelies'.

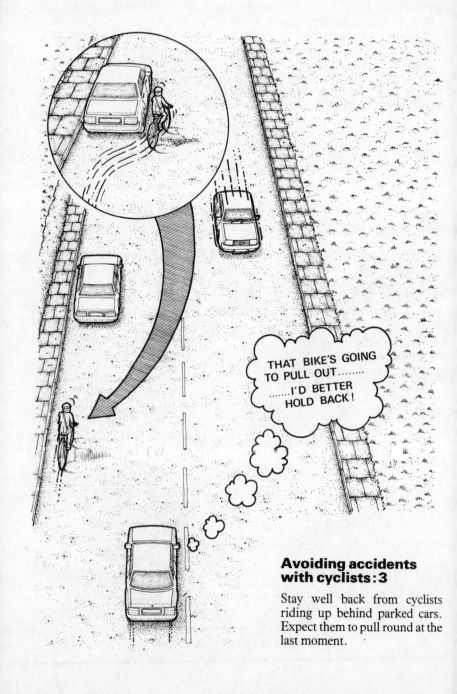

Avoiding accidents with cyclists: 3

Stay well back from cyclists riding up behind parked cars. Expect them to pull round at the last moment.

When in doubt, avoid overtaking: 1

Overtaking is one of the most dangerous manoeuvres. Decide if the benefits are worth the risks involved. There is little point in it if you are soon to turn off or there is a long line of traffic ahead.

What if . . . the other driver pulls out to pass a cyclist or parked car just ahead which you haven't noticed? Is the other driver turning off? Is anyone overtaking you?

THAT DRIVER BEHIND'S THINKING OF OVERTAKING ME!

IT LOOKS SAFE TO GET BY NOW....

When in doubt, avoid overtaking : 2

To overtake safely you need a long straight stretch of fairly wide road free of oncoming vehicles, obstructions and side turns. To get a good view, stay well back and look along the nearside. Move over until you can see along the offside.

Be prepared to engage a lower gear and accelerate quickly. You may need a signal.

After overtaking, pull back onto your own side as soon as you can without cutting in.

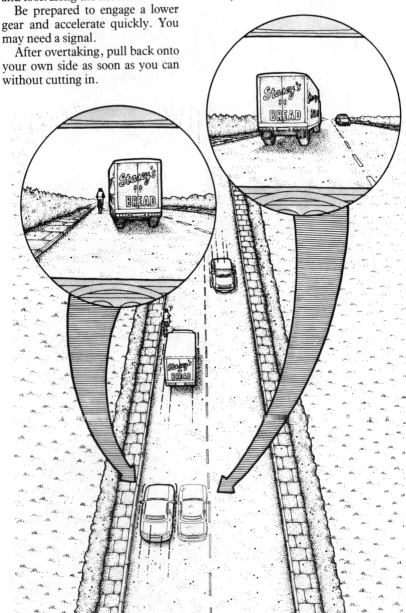

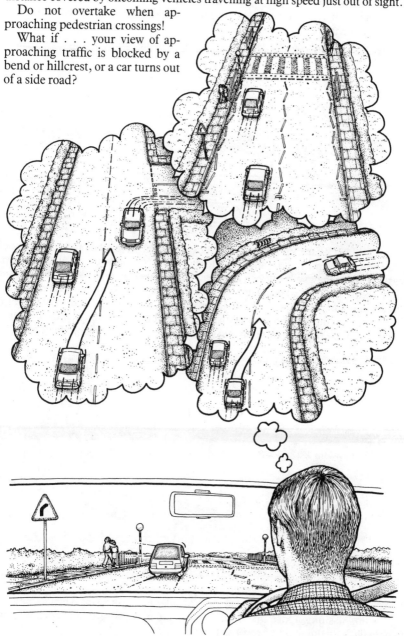

When in doubt, avoid overtaking:3

Think about the distance you will travel whilst overtaking. Think about the distance covered by oncoming vehicles travelling at high speed just out of sight.

Do not overtake when approaching pedestrian crossings!

What if . . . your view of approaching traffic is blocked by a bend or hillcrest, or a car turns out of a side road?

Avoiding accidents at pedestrian crossings: 1

Look well ahead for people standing near or within reaching distance of crossings. Decide whether they are likely to cross and be ready to slow down. You *must* give precedence to anyone with a foot on the crossing. What if . . . someone steps out at the last moment?

If you hold back early enough, pedestrians will usually cross before you reach the give way lines and reduce the need to stop. Try to make eye contact to help reassure them they've been seen and that you are likely to give them precedence. Allow extra time for old or infirm people and those with prams or small children. Be cautious and patient with children and teenagers! Some may dash straight onto the crossing at the last moment whilst others deliberately saunter across to make you wait. Don't retaliate by going too close, moving off too soon or too quickly.

If your view of the pavement is blocked slow down, as you would if someone was crossing, until you can see it is safe to continue. Always park well away from any kind of pedestrian crossing!

At pelican crossings give precedence to people already crossing when the amber light starts flashing. Once they have crossed you may proceed but watch out for people dashing out and be prepared to let them go.

Avoiding accidents at pedestrian crossings: 2

Do not overtake approaching a crossing. In lanes you may pull up level with the leading vehicle but do not pass it. Where there is a refuge in the middle, look for pedestrians on the other side nearing the central reserve. They may not realise it is classed as two separate crossings and walk straight through.

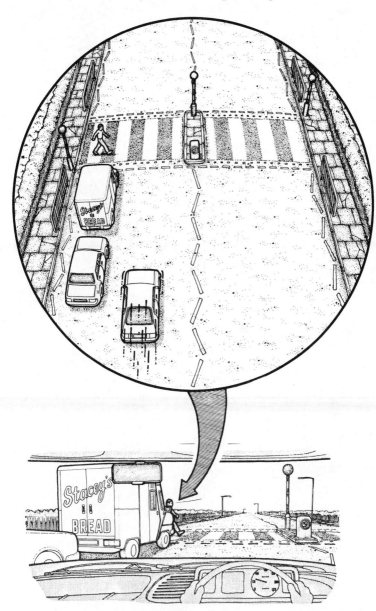

Avoiding accidents at pedestrian crossings: 3

The timing at some traffic lights incorporating pedestrian crossings does not always allow sufficient time for right-turning drivers to clear the junction.

You must wait for oncoming vehicles before you can clear the junction, by which time the green man may be on. Start to clear the junction as soon as you can but look out for people using the crossing.

Pull forwards into this position and wait until they are safely across.

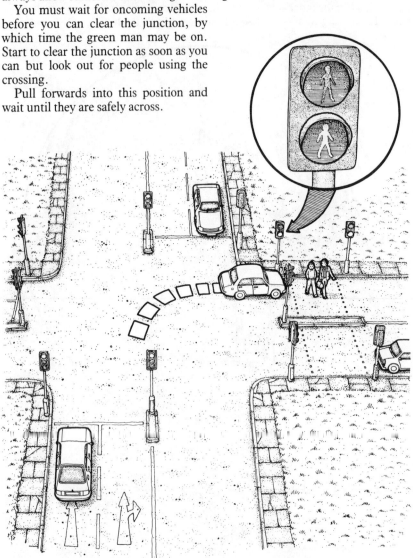

How to avoid accidents near parked vehicles

Look for signs of movement through the windows and for feet underneath. Watch for doors opening and people getting in or out. What if . . . another driver moves out of a side road because their view of you is also blocked?

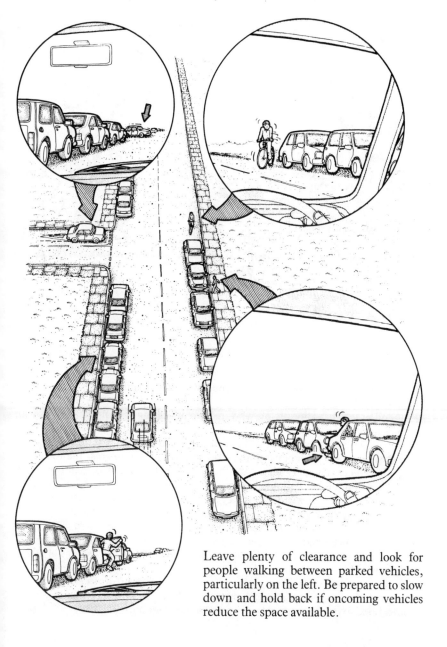

Leave plenty of clearance and look for people walking between parked vehicles, particularly on the left. Be prepared to slow down and hold back if oncoming vehicles reduce the space available.

How to avoid accidents with pedestrians : 1

Two out of every three pedestrians killed or seriously injured are either under 15 or over 60. People in these age groups may misjudge your speed and distance. What if . . . they step out into the road?

Be patient with old people who tend to be slow and hesitant. Show extra care to the disabled and infirm. Look out for people with white walking sticks or guide dogs. Remember too that some people who are hard of hearing or deaf will not hear your vehicle approaching.

Slow down and drive further away from the kerb in busy pedestrian areas and expect shoppers to step out into the road. Expect people to cross the road near junctions and corners. Watch out for them walking between parked or stationary vehicles or hidden behind mobile shops. Leave plenty of clearance when passing and approach at a safe speed where they are in or near the road. Check your mirror and be ready to stop if necessary. Be prepared to sound your horn to inform them of your presence. Do this as a friendly warning and never to tell them off.

In wet weather avoid driving through puddles and spraying pedestrians. Reduce speed if they can't be avoided! Drive with consideration for the feelings of others and proper care for their safety.

When turning across a footpath to move into a drive or works entrance, you must 'give way' to pedestrians walking along it. When driving across the pavement from a blind exit, go slow and be prepared to tap your horn lightly.

How to avoid accidents with pedestrians: 2

Where pedestrians are walking or standing close to the kerb check your mirrors and be prepared to move further out as you approach them.

Drive slowly near schools, particularly at the times when children come and go. Be extra careful near ice cream vans and where you see very small children not restrained or holding someone's hand.

Children are quick and impulsive. They are usually too busy playing to notice what you are doing and they can move unexpectedly. Be prepared to stop! As you approach them, check on following traffic and slow down to a speed at which you can pull up if one runs out.

If you can do so safely, be prepared to make adjustments to your course. Even slight deviations give more clearance and extra time in an emergency.

How to avoid accidents with pedestrians: 3

In icy weather pedestrians frequently walk in the road to avoid slipping on pavements. Try to be understanding and make allowances. Joggers too seem to insist on running in the road. Watch out for them, particularly at night when they can be very difficult to see. If they are wearing dark tracksuits it is even harder to see them, even on lit roads.

Expect people walking in, or crossing, the road just out of sight round bends or over hillcrests, especially when driving on country roads with no footpaths.

Check on following traffic and be prepared to slow down. Be ready to pull up if necessary or move round them.

How to avoid accidents with emerging vehicles

Approaching side roads, try to make eye contact with any drivers waiting to pull out. At least then you can be sure they've seen you. Watch out for any approaching too fast. What if . . . they pull out?

There may be junctions hidden behind parked vehicles. Remember the view of emerging drivers will be restricted. Cover the brake pedal ready for action even though you have the right of way.

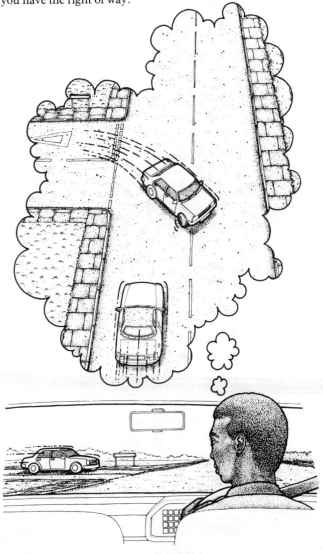

Avoiding accidents with animals

When you see them, assess the risk, check on following traffic and be prepared to slow down. What if . . . one runs out? Keep both hands on the wheel, hold the steering on a straight course and brake firmly.

Hold well back from horses until you can leave enough room for passing safely. Avoid passing at speed with a high revving engine and don't use the horn!

How to avoid accidents on country roads

The countryside holds its own special dangers. Drive slowly on narrow roads, through villages and near farm entrances. Take extra care at lambing time and when driving through country parks.

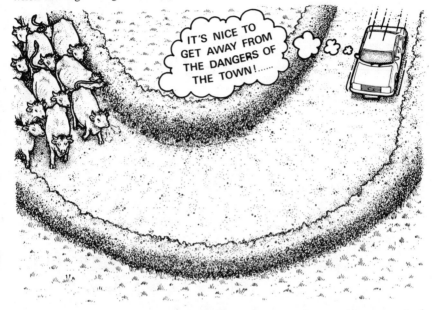

Drive slowly on muddy roads and where your view is restricted. Expect to find obstructions such as slower moving agricultural vehicles and pedestrians walking in the road. Be patient if you get stuck behind a slow moving vehicle on a narrow road. When it is obviously unsafe to overtake it is not worth the frustration and risk involved in trying.

Expect sharp bends, mud on the road and tractors pulling into the road from fields and farmyards. On narrow single-track roads keep your speed down and be prepared to give way to oncoming traffic. Wait in or opposite a passing place.

How to avoid accidents with vehicles at your sides

Avoid driving in the blind spots of drivers at your sides. Stay back from the vehicle ahead especially when negotiating a curved course.

Drivers of large vehicles may need to steer an unusual course through some junctions. Expect them to swing out before turning left or position close to the left before turning right into a factory entrance or narrow road.

The sheer size of the vehicle may mean the driver has no option but to cut corners or take an unusual course through a roundabout.

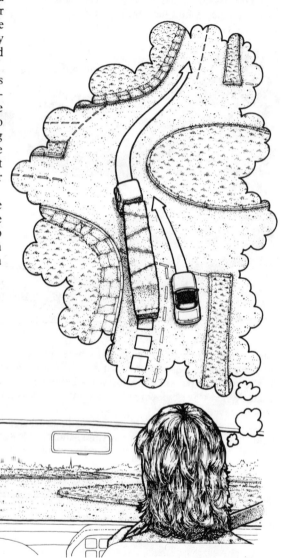

Avoiding collisions turning on to dual carriageways

Decide if there is enough room in the opening to offer protection from traffic moving along the dual carriageway.

Avoiding accidents when manoeuvring

Before reversing, check to the front, rear and sides for other road users and obstructions. Turn well round in your seat until you can see clearly where you are going. Keep a special lookout for pedestrians before you start. Move very slowly, particularly if people are standing nearby or if your view is at all restricted. Keep looking all around for approaching traffic as you manoeuvre.

Avoid reversing from side roads into main roads; or manoeuvres such as the three point and U turns on busy roads where they will inconvenience or endanger others. When reversing out of driveways across the pavement look out for pedestrians, move back very slowly and keep checking for them.

Check blind spots before moving off and opening doors

Before opening a door to get out, check the blind spot. Before driving away again, take an initial look to the front and in the mirrors as you get ready to move. To be 100% sure it's safe to move away, check the blind spots and be prepared to wait.

When leaving your vehicle, it is always safer to find an off-road parking position. Lock valuables in the boot and make sure all the windows and doors are properly secured.

Don't be a danger to others!

Park well away from bends, junctions, hilltops and any other place where the view of other drivers is restricted. Inconsiderate parking forces other drivers on to the wrong side when approaching traffic is hidden from view. As additional precautions when parking on steep hills, leave the vehicle in first or reverse gear and point the wheels in towards the kerb.

Find a legal position to park on a straight part of the road. Stop well away from any vehicles parked on the opposite side. Park away from schools and do not block entrances to hospitals, fire stations, doctors and private drives.

The parking brake must be applied before you leave your vehicle. Whilst driving you should put it on whenever you are stationary, or waiting for something or someone longer than the time it takes to comfortably put it on and release it again without delaying your progress.

5 Advanced Driving Tests and Training

The RoSPA Advanced Driving Test

RoSPA advanced tests are conducted at locations all over the UK by police class 1 drivers and last about 1¼ hours. The cost is currently £18 and includes the first year's membership of the RoSPA Advanced Drivers Association. Subsequent annual subscriptions are £10.

RoSPA have a unique system of grading successful candidates into grades 1, 2 and 3, which seems to be a fairer way of assessing performance over a wider range of driving ability. It provides incentives for the less experienced seeking to improve on their standard continuously and, at the same time, gives a meaningful measure of attainment to the more skilful driver. Grade 1 is the highest and it is unlikely that anyone will achieve this without a thorough knowledge of *Roadcraft*, the police drivers' manual, and the system of car control it advocates.

Applying for the test

Application forms can be obtained from:
The Administrative Officer,
RoSPA Advanced Drivers Association,
Cannon House,
The Priory, Queensway,
Birmingham B4 6BS.
Tel: 021–200 2461.

The test

Cars used for the test must be in a roadworthy condition and the candidate's visibility must not be obscured by condensation or for other reasons. Examiners will take a serious view of candidates who, for example on a rainy day, attempt to drive whilst visibility is restricted by condensation on windows and mirrors. Proper use of the wipers, demisters and window winder are expected.

The use of the controls

At the start of the test examiners try to put candidates at ease.

Before starting off, candidates are required to carry out the cockpit drill followed by a brake test shortly after moving.

Candidates are expected to demonstrate their mechanical appreciation by controlling the vehicle smoothly. Examiners will assess the steering method and position of the hands and arms when turning the wheel. The clutch should be used smoothly. Single de-clutching is acceptable but examiners will be pleased to see double de-clutching where appropriate. Slipping and riding the clutch is frowned upon. Examiners will assess the position of the hand on the gear lever when executing selections, the matching of engine revolutions to road speed and the correct timing of gear changes. The intelligent use of intermediate gears will make a difference to the final grade achieved. The use of the brakes is assessed for smoothness, early braking in correct sequence relating to the 'system', skid avoidance through correct technique and progressive reduction in pedal pressure as the vehicle is brought to a smooth stop. The accelerator should be used firmly when needed, precisely and under control at all times. Acceleration sense in overtaking will be assessed along with anticipation and the smooth variation of speeds to meet changing road and traffic conditions without braking.

Candidates are expected to use the mirrors in the correct sequence and have an accurate and continuous knowledge of the traffic situation behind. Over the shoulder looks are expected at appropriate times. Candidates are also assessed in their use of the horn.

Driving performance

Moving off and stopping should be smooth and carried out safely. Examiners will assess the correct application of the system of car control, whether candidates brake before or after changing gear and whether they signal too late or too early. Particular emphasis is placed on the way the vehicle is positioned at junctions, on the approach to roundabouts, on the open road and in lanes on the approach to hazards.

Candidates will be assessed on their course when cornering and whether the line taken optimises visibility and safety and that it allows for any tendency of the vehicle to over- or understeer to be compensated for. The use of speed and vehicle controls will be assessed whilst cornering.

Candidates will be assessed on whether necessary signals are omitted or wrongly timed and unnecessary ones used. The examiner will look for reinforcement of trafficators by an arm signal where necessary and assess reactions to traffic signs.

Candidates are required to perform a reversing exercise safely and accurately and in normal driving to make reasonable use of their vehicle's performance within legal limits and as safety allows according to the prevailing road and traffic conditions. Examiners will assess whether candidates are asking themselves the appropriate questions before executing an overtaking manoeuvre.

General ability

Candidates who are slumped at the wheel or resting an elbow on the door will not be considered as advanced drivers. Consideration for others and self-control will be assessed. Temperament whilst driving should be calm, relaxed and decisive.

Candidates are not expected to abuse their vehicles by 'kerbing', etc.

Examiners will assess candidates' powers of observation, hazard recognition and planning. Candidates may, if they choose, elect to give a commentary drive if invited to 'think aloud' for a few minutes by the examiner. Candidates will also be assessed on their ability to judge their own speed and the speeds and distances of other vehicles. This will be linked to candidates' use of braking and acceleration.

The test is concluded with questions on the Highway Code and other motoring matters such as those contained in most vehicle handbooks.

After the test

The examiner will discuss any points that have arisen and inform candidates whether they have passed and which grade they have achieved. Persons attaining grades 1 and 2 are expected to take a refresher test at three-yearly intervals. The fee for this is included in the yearly subscriptions. Grade 3 candidates are expected to take the test every year until they are upgraded. Candidates who fail the test are permitted to retake it after three months.

RoSPA defensive driving courses

RoSPA development of defensive driving stems from the organised road accident prevention work which the society has undertaken since 1918 and forms a significant element of its efforts to reduce the high level of deaths and injuries on the roads of Britain.

The importance of training drivers may be judged from current accident levels. Each year on our roads around 6,000 people are killed and a further 300,000 injured, at an estimated cost to the community of £2,000 million. In over 95% of these accidents, human error has been shown to be the major factor. Given that the majority of road mileage is undertaken on business journeys, it is easy to see how helping the drivers of company vehicles to improve their performance can significantly improve the situation.

Cost-effectiveness is an important consideration whenever decisions are made on the expenditure of limited resources. In this context, it is important to remember the cost savings, particularly in the field of insurance premiums, which can be achieved by organisations which take serious steps to help their own staff secure improved standards in the driving task.

The RoSPA training service operates at two levels: in the classroom and in the vehicle. The classroom-based course, usually conducted as in-company training, is an intensive one-day session which will accommodate up to 15 students and aims to impart the basic theory of defensive driving. This session is aimed at increasing the driver's knowledge of advanced and defensive principles.

On-road training is achieved by taking groups of drivers out for the day in their company vehicle. In addition to observing a demonstration drive by the instructor, each student takes a turn at the wheel and all are encouraged to learn from each other's mistakes and the corrective tuition applied. In this way, drivers are helped with the difficult task of adapting their own driving technique in the light of the theoretical knowledge they have gained.

The course aims to increase awareness of accident potential and improve the driver's attitude to the task and includes a comprehensive defensive driving manual covering speed and overtaking, drink, drugs and driving, turning and cornering, night driving, observation, the law, aquaplaning and skidding, winter driving, roadcraft, the vehicle, signs and signals, stopping and parking, passenger safety, accidents, motorway driving, first aid, the heavy goods vehicle and a revision guide.

In addition to company training, RoSPA, in association with the Motor Schools Association, maintain a register of persons qualified to provide training linked to the advanced test syllabus. Instructors with their names on this register have all attended and passed a special three-day Diploma course in advanced driver instruction. Instructors requiring additional information about the register should either contact RoSPA direct or contact the Motor Schools Association.

The society are also seeking to extend the availability of courses throughout the country and to this end have developed a Better Driving Course Syllabus Pack. This contains teaching notes, a master syllabus, a list of recommended resource materials and further guidance notes for use by road safety officers, police officers, approved driving instructors and others conducting better driving courses. The course consists of six two-hour sessions in the classroom with provision for an assessment drive with one of the local group associations. The society also maintains a register of their local advanced driving groups from which these packs can be obtained. These groups can also offer associate membership and provide help and advice to candidates before they take the RoSPA Advanced Driving Test.

The Institute of Advanced Motorists

Application forms can be obtained from:
The Institute of Advanced Motorists,
IAM House,
359 Chiswick High Road,
London W4 4HS.
Tel: 01–994 4403.
The test costs £24 (includes annual subscription for first year of £7.50). It is conducted by class 1 police drivers in over 90 towns throughout the country. The test lasts for around 90 minutes on a route of about 35 to 40 miles. This covers a wide range of traffic conditions on both rural and urban roads. Candidates will be expected to make reasonable use of their vehicle's performance within the speed limits and normal parameters of safety with regard to the road, traffic and weather conditions. Candidates are expected to reverse into a side road and execute a hill start and will be assessed on their powers of observation.
of observation.

The test is something which any driver with a reasonable amount of experience and skill should be able to pass without too much difficulty. Candidates do not fail for committing minor faults. Even those who do fail should learn some important lessons from the examiner conducting the test. Successful candidates may:

- display the Institute's badge on their car;
- take advantage of special insurance terms;
- receive *Milestones*, the motoring magazine specially written for those with a keen interest in driving;
- join their local IAM group and participate in the road safety, driving and social events which they organise.

During the test

Examiners look for the following points:

- *Acceleration* – this should be smooth and progressive. It should be used at the right time in the right places. Acceleration should be neither excessive nor insufficient.

- *Braking* – this should be smooth and progressive. Brakes should be used in conjunction with the mirror and signals. They should not be used late or fiercely. Candidates will be expected to take account of the road conditions.
- *Clutch control* – the engine and road speeds must be properly co-ordinated when changing gear. Candidates should not slip or ride the clutch, nor should they coast with the clutch disengaged.
- *Gear changing* – changes should be selected smoothly and fluently. If automatic transmission is fitted, candidates should make full use of it.
- *Use of gears* – candidates must make correct use of the gears. The correct gear should be selected before reaching a hazard.
- *Steering* – the wheel should be held correctly with the hands at the quarter to three or ten to two position. The use of the crossed arm technique, except when manoeuvring in a confined space, is not recommended by the Institute.
- *Seating position* – candidates should be alert and not slumped at the wheel. They should not rest an arm on the door whilst driving.
- *Observation* – candidates should read the road well ahead and anticipate the actions of other road users. They must be able to judge correctly the speeds and distances of other vehicles.
- *Concentration* – candidates should concentrate on the road and traffic situation and not allow themselves to be easily distracted.
- *Maintaining progress* – with regard to the road, traffic and weather conditions, candidates should make use of their vehicle's performance by driving at a reasonable pace, maintaining good progress throughout.
- *Obstruction* – candidates should not obstruct other road users by driving too slowly, by positioning incorrectly on the road or by failing to anticipate and react correctly to the traffic situation ahead.
- *Positioning* – candidates should keep in the correct part of the road, especially when approaching and negotiating hazards.
- *Lane discipline* – candidates should drive in the appropriate lane and be careful not to straddle white lines.
- *Observation of surfaces* – candidates should continually assess the road surface, especially in poor weather, and look out for slippery conditions.
- *Traffic signals* – candidates must observe and respond correctly to signals, signs and road markings and extend proper courtesies at pedestrian crossings.
- *Speed limits and other legal requirements* – these must be observed at all times.
- *Overtaking* – candidates must overtake safely whilst maintaining a correct distance from other vehicles and using the mirrors, signals and gears correctly.
- *Hazard procedure and cornering* – candidates must have full control over their vehicle on the approach to hazards. They must negotiate them in the correct position, driving at an appropriate speed with a suitable gear engaged.
- *Mirror* – mirrors should be used frequently, especially before signalling and making changes to speed or course.
- *Signals* – signals given by direction indicator, or arm if required, should be given in the right place and in good time. The horn and headlight flasher should only be used in accordance with the Highway Code.

- *Restraint* – candidates should display reasonable restraint, without being indecisive.
- *Consideration* – candidates should extend consideration and courtesy to other road users.
- *Car sympathy* – candidates should not over-stress the vehicle, for example by revving the engine needlessly or by fierce braking.
- *Manoeuvres* – these should be carried out smoothly and competently.

Reasons for failure

78% *Hazard procedure and cornering:* incorrect assessment; poor safety margins; unsystematic procedure.

72% *Use of gears:* late selection; intermediate gears not used to advantage.

70% *Positioning:* straddling lanes; incorrect position for right or left turns.

60% *Braking:* late application; harsh handbrake application; braking and gear changing simultaneously.

58% *Distance observation:* late planning and assessment of traffic conditions.

48% *Method of approach:* too fast; coasted to compulsory stop; offside at 'keep left' sign.

48% *Clutch control:* riding; slipping; coasting.

40% *Car sympathy:* not expressed in use of clutch, brakes or gears.

38% *Gear changing:* harsh selection; changing down with relaxed accelerator.

38% *Traffic observation:* poor anticipation; late reaction.

38% *Overtaking:* too close prior to; on bends; in face of oncoming vehicles; cutting in after completing manoeuvre.

36% *Observation and obedience:* failing to specify requested signs; failure to conform to stop sign/keep left signs and markings.

28% *Manoeuvring and reversing:* lacked judgement and control.

26% *Correct use of speed:* excessive in country lanes; failing to make adequate progress in 70 mph areas.

22% *Speed limits:* exceeding limit.

20% *Steering:* released wheel; crossed hands.

20% *Restraint:* insufficient restraint demonstrated.

14% *Maintaining adequate progress:* not maintained when safe to make progress.

14% *Hand or mechanical signals:* late or misleading.

14% *Correct use of the horn:* not used when required.

12% *Acceleration:* poor acceleration sense.

8% *Obstructing other vehicles:* loitering at minor hazards and cutting in.

Defensive driving courses

Selecting safer drivers can reduce the running costs for fleet operators with savings to be made from lower motoring expenses and insurance premiums. Autodriva courses provide groups of three employees with an intensive one-day in-car session designed to sharpen awareness, improve vehicle sympathy and reduce the risk of accident involvement. Practical demonstration drives on the early recognition of risk potential and the need to compensate for the actions of others are reinforced with practical hands-on experience.

Additional specialised packages include a half-day skid prevention and control course and company days which include the skid prevention and control course and a special high performance course at Goodwood motor circuit.

Autodriva developed a structured programme for teaching students to drive in schools and colleges which, during field trials, achieved L test pass rates of over double the national average. This was later restructured to form the basis of the National Joint Council of Approved Driving Instructor Organisations staff tutors' courses. The authors of this book, as well as of *The Driving Instructor's Handbook* and *Learn to Drive*, are staff instructors who have helped to influence new standards of driving instruction both at home and abroad. Nigel Stacey was instrumental in the development of an advanced examination syllabus for instructors. Further details from:

Autodriva Training Systems,
The Vine,
Chapel Saint Leonards,
Lincolnshire PE24 5TH.
Tel: (0754) 72228.

Registration of approved driving instructors

It is an offence to teach another person to drive a motor car for profit or reward (maximum penalty £1,000) unless the supervisor:

    a. is on the Department of Transport Approved Driving Instructor Register;
    b. holds a licence to give instruction issued by the Registrar.

Applications

All forms concerned with applications for names to be placed on the register, examination appointments and licences to instruct should be obtained from your local traffic area office. Registration is normally for four years, renewable on application and payment of a further fee. Qualifying applicants are entitled to receive an official Certificate of Registration and call themselves 'Department of Transport Approved Driving Instructors'. To qualify for the Register applicants must:

    i. have held a *full* car driving licence for periods totalling at least four years out of the *six* years preceding the date of application
      (provisional licences do not qualify but periods after passing the driving test may be counted towards the four years out of the previous six)
    ii. not have been under a disqualification from driving for any part of the *four* years preceding the date of application
    iii. be a fit and proper person to have his/her name entered in the Register
      (all motoring and non-motoring offences, providing they are not 'spent' under the Rehabilitation of Offenders Act 1974, will be taken into account in assessing an applicant's suitability)
    iv. pass the Register qualifying examinations.

The ADI Register qualifying examinations

The examination is in three separate parts. Part 1 is a test of theory. Part 2 is a practical test of driving ability (includes tests of eyesight and driving technique). Part 3 is a practical test of instructional ability.

Applicants must pass each part of the examination in the above sequence before applying for the next. To qualify, applicants must pass all three elements within a two-year period. Where candidates fail to do this they must start again from the beginning and pass them all again.

Applicants are advised to seek professional guidance before sitting the Part 1 test of theory and attend properly structured courses before taking the Part 2 and Part 3 tests. Applicants can apply to take each of the tests at any centre of their choice. Applications for the tests should be made to the appropriate traffic area office.

Part 1: test of theory is conducted in: London, Aberdeen, Birmingham, Bristol, Cambridge, Cardiff, Chatham, Chelmsford, Chester, Eastbourne, Edinburgh, Glasgow, Inverness, Leeds, Manchester, Newcastle-upon-Tyne, Nottingham, Oxford, Plymouth, Preston and Southampton.

Parts 2 and 3: tests of driving and instructional ability are conducted at: Bridgend, Bristol, Cambridge, Chester, Coventry, Darlington, Dartford, Eastbourne, Edinburgh, Epping, Glasgow, Guildford, Hull, Inverness, Isleworth, Leeds, Liverpool, Maidstone, Manchester, Newcastle-upon-Tyne, Northampton, Norwich, Nottingham, Oxford, Plymouth, Preston, Redhill, Sheffield, Southampton, Taunton, Watford, Wolverhampton and Worcester.

When attending for the Parts 2 and 3 tests candidates must provide a suitable saloon or estate car in which to take the test. The vehicle must:

 i. be in a roadworthy and proper condition and capable of normal performance for a vehicle of its type;
 ii. have an orthodox manual transmission system;
 iii. have right-hand drive steering;
 iv. have a readily adjustable driving seat and forward facing passenger seat;
 v. be properly insured and cover the examiner for all third party and damage risks and his liability to any passenger;
 vi. during the Part 2 test of driving technique not display any advertisements or signs which might cause others to believe it is being used for driving instruction.

In addition, candidates attending for the Part 3 test must have two regulation L plates which they can attach to the vehicle.

The Part 1 test of theory

The Part 1 test of theory consists of a single 1½ hour paper of 100 multiple choice questions. Candidates are usually notified of the result within two weeks. This test requires a high standard of knowledge on the following subjects:

 a. the principles of road safety in general and their application in specified circumstances;
 b. correct and courteous driving techniques including:
    - control of the vehicle,
    - road procedure,
    - hazard recognition and proper action,
    - dealing properly with other road users and pedestrians,

- the use of safety equipment;
c. the tuition required to instruct a pupil in driving a car, the correction of errors, the manner of the instructor, instructor/student relationships, and vehicle adaptations for disabled drivers;
d. the Highway Code and other matters included in the booklet in which it is contained;
e. the DTp pamphlet 'Your Driving Test';
f. the interpretation of the DTp pamphlet ('The Statement of Failure to Pass the Driving Test');
g. adequate knowledge of the mechanisms and design of a motor car relating to driving instruction;
h. the book *Driving* (the official Department of Transport manual).

The Part 2 test of driving ability

This includes a test of eyesight and a test of driving technique.

The eyesight test requires candidates to read a number plate at 90 feet for symbols three and one eighth inches in height and 100 feet for symbols three and one half inches in height. Candidates who fail this are not allowed to continue with the test of driving technique.

The test of driving technique is of about one hour's duration. A high standard is expected and candidates are assessed as experienced drivers. Those who incur more than six recorded faults or one or more serious faults automatically fail. Routes will be varied to take in both urban and rural areas. Candidates are expected to make reasonable lawful use of the vehicle's performance and satisfy the examiner on all or any of the following subjects:

a. expert handling of the controls of the vehicle
b. correct use of road procedures
c. anticipation of the actions of others and taking appropriate action
d. sound judgement of distance, speed and timing
e. consideration for the safety of other road users.

Candidates are expected to perform all or any of the following exercises:

f. move away straight ahead or at an angle
g. overtake, meet or cross the path of other vehicles and take an appropriate course
h. turn right-hand and left-hand corners correctly
i. stop the vehicle as in an emergency
j. drive the vehicle backwards and whilst so doing enter limited openings to the right and to the left; and
k. cause the vehicle to face in the opposite direction by the use of forward and reverse gears.

The Part 3 test of instructional ability

This assesses the candidate's instructional ability and the technical correctness of the instruction given. Candidates are expected to demonstrate their ability to instruct learner drivers at different stages of tuition. The test consists of two phases. Phase 1 involves giving instruction to a complete beginner or a learner with some experience. Phase 2 involves giving tuition to a learner at about driving test standard.

Each phase is of about 30 minutes' duration. In each the examiner will give the candidate a briefing and short description of the learner to whom instruction must be given. The examiner will then simulate the role of the learner described in the briefing. Candidates should listen carefully to the briefing and background detail given by the examiner. They are expected to cover the subject area specified by the examiner at a level of instruction that is appropriate for the description of the learner. During the test the examiner will also be looking at various other aspects of the candidate's performance. These include characteristics such as patience, tact, firmness and enthusiasm as well as the overall confidence and general manner of the candidate.

Training to qualify as a driving instructor

Autodriva (see address on page 118) provide experienced drivers with a comprehensive three-part course specially structured to enable them to concentrate on passing one part of the examination at a time. A home study programme systematically prepares candidates for the Part 1 ADI exam in the privacy of their own homes. Practical training is organised in two parts for the test of driving technique and instructional ability. Advice and practical assistance is also available to successful candidates wishing to start up their own business. The complete kit includes five structured workbooks and a comprehensive support pack containing study instructions; special notes; self-test checkpoints; mock exam papers; more than 700 multiple choice questions; a structured guide for teaching learner drivers; a practical guide to the Part 2 test of driving ability; the Highway Code; DL68; and The Driving Manual.

Each course workbook contains a number of study units. The study units contain instructions which refer to the relevant reference materials. At the end of each study unit there are self-test checkpoints. These contain up to 26 multiple choice questions similar to those used in the examination. They inform candidates of progress and help reassure them as they work through the course.

The Autodriva syllabus provides a properly structured and comprehensive course linked to Department of Transport requirements.

Heavy goods vehicle and public service vehicle driving licences

The minimum standards for drivers of heavy goods vehicles and public service vehicles are higher than for drivers of cars and light goods vehicles, and licences are issued only to applicants who are acceptable to the licensing authority. For example, previous driving history and offences relating to drivers' hours and/or loading of vehicles may be taken into account when considering the issue or renewal of a licence, especially after a period of disqualification.

Initial applications for licences must be accompanied by an official medical report form (DTp 20003) and this must be signed by a registered medical practitioner. Licences will be refused if, for example:

- you have had an epileptic attack since you reached the age of 5
- you have had a coronary thrombosis or heart surgery
- you suffer from problems of heart rhythm or disease of the heart or arteries
- you are treated with certain drugs for high blood pressure
- you need injections of insulin for diabetes
- you have had a stroke, unexplained loss of consciousness, severe head injury with continuing after-effects, or major brain surgery
- you suffer from Parkinson's disease or multiple sclerosis
- you are being treated for mental or nervous problems
- you have had drink or drug problems or suffered mental illness in recent years
- your hearing is so bad that you cannot use the telephone in an emergency
- you have any other condition which makes vocational driving inadvisable.

In addition, you must be able to see with both eyes and not suffer from double or tunnel vision or other eye trouble which might make you unfit to drive vocationally.

The HGV driving test

An HGV driver's licence is required to drive any articulated vehicle or any other vehicle constructed to carry or haul goods and which exceeds the permissible maximum weight of 7.5 tonnes.

Applications should be made to the traffic area office. The HGV tests are conducted at special centres, which have an off-road manoeuvring site, by very experienced and specially trained examiners. The design and construction of modern heavy goods vehicles demands especially high standards and skills from those who drive them. The purpose of the HGV test is to ensure that those who want to drive them have the necessary ability to ensure they are driven with the utmost safety, courtesy and consideration for all other road users.

Candidates must satisfy the examiner that they are able to control and handle the vehicle safely whatever the conditions. The test includes reversing and braking exercises which are carried out on a special paved area at the test centre. Because of the size, special handling characteristics, and the restrictions to vision at the rear and sides, candidates should pay particular attention to: pre-starting checks; safety of moving off; proper use of the vehicle controls; proper use of interior and exterior mirrors and rear observations; appropriate use of signals; proper care in the use of speed; maintaining a safe separation distance from the vehicle ahead; proper observations and care when turning; overtaking/meeting and crossing the path of other vehicles safely; alertness and anticipation of others' actions; the use of motorways.

Candidates will be tested on their knowledge of the Highway Code, vehicle operation, actions required in the event of malfunctions to critical systems, and the effects of load distribution. Drivers of articulated vehicles will be tested on their knowledge of un-coupling and re-coupling the trailer.

The PSV driving test

A PSV driver's licence is required to drive a bus carrying fare-paying passengers. Applications should be made to the traffic commissioners at the main traffic area offices or, in the case of the metropolitan area, to the commissioner of police for the metropolis. There is no provisional PSV licence as training is carried out in an empty bus. The training vehicle is driven on an ordinary licence. The application for the licence is made at the same time as the application for a test. Initial applications should include a medical form signed by a registered medical practitioner, an ordinary driving licence, a PSV licence application and fee and the PSV test application and fee.

PSV tests are conducted at HGV driving test centres. The test lasts about 1½ hours and is similar to the HGV test. Its purpose is to assess the driver's competence to drive a PSV in a manner which shows consideration to the safety and comfort of passengers and without danger to others.

The test includes off-road reversing and braking exercises. During the on-road section the safety and comfort of passengers should be reflected in the candidate's smooth use of the controls and steering. Candidates should not strike the kerb nor mount the pavement *unless* this is necessary due to the large size of the vehicle and restricted space in which to manoeuvre. Under such circumstances, it must be *safe* and executed sympathetically. The test includes: a downhill start; an uphill start ('snatch' gear change may be needed uphill); gear change exercises up and down, and parking at a bus stop.

The test includes oral questions on the Highway Code, road signs and markings, vehicle safety, PSV regulations and safety equipment.

HGV and PSV driver training

The training for HGV and PSV driving instructors is carried out by the Road Transport Industry Training Board at centres at High Ercall, Shropshire and Livingston, Scotland. Details of the facilities available may be obtained from RTITB at Wembley. HGV and PSV driver training is available from a variety of sources. The RTITB have several group training associations at centres in all areas and there are many commercial driving schools at different locations. For further information on training contact Jem Ballantyne at:

Miller Transport Training,
Goodwood Motor Circuit,
Nr Chichester,
West Sussex PO18 0PH.
Tel: (0243) 783540/784715.

Motor racing

To race competitively you will require a competition licence from the RAC and a medical certificate; membership of a recognised racing club (such as the British Automobile Racing Club); and a car which complies with the RAC regulations for racing. Anyone wanting to take up motor racing should first consider taking lessons.

Public roads are not the right place for the competitive spirit and any aspirations you may have in this direction should be channelled towards motor sport.

Application forms for the racing drivers' course can be obtained from:

Jim Russell International Racing Drivers' School,
Snetterton Circuit,
Norwich,
Norfolk NR16 2JX.
Tel: (095 387) 8428.

Day one of this eight-day course is spent on introductions and medicals. In the evening there is a welcoming party. Day 2 is spent on skid control training in saloon vehicles on the school's own special circuit. Day 3 provides pupils with the introductory trial and corner tuition designed to familiarise them with the handling, gear changing, braking and steering of the Formula Ford single-seater racing cars. Days 4 and 5 are spent lapping the circuit under the strict supervision of the instructors. Day 6 is spent back on the skid control circuit in single-seaters and on visits to the nearby Lotus factory or observing top European drivers testing cars on the circuit. Day 7 is spent lapping the circuit at increased rev limits culminating in the top limits. Day 8 is race day. The morning practice session decides the grid positions for the afternoon course races. The main object is to attain the first signature on his/her licence from the official RAC steward. The culmination is the prize giving, where successful pupils receive a graduation diploma and where trophies are awarded to the race winners.

Racing and speed trials

A person who promotes, or takes part in, a race or trial of speed between motor vehicles on a public road is guilty of an offence. A person who promotes or takes part in a competition or trial, involving the use of motor vehicles on a public road, is also guilty of an offence unless the event is authorised and conducted in accordance with regulations.

Permitted events include those where the number of vehicles does not exceed 12, subject to other conditions; those which attach no merit to the lowest mileage, contain no performance tests or specified routes; those where merit, attached to competitors' performance relates only to good road behaviour in compliance with the Highway Code; those designated solely to training members of the armed forces; those authorised by the RAC in accordance with the Motor Vehicles (Competition and Trials) Regulations 1969.

Autocross: events exist on grass or similar farmland surfaces for amateurs with road cars. Competitors may be started individually and timed over a standing start lap, followed by a flying start lap. Cars may be started in pairs or more.

Autotests: these consist of a series of specified manoeuvres which must be completed in sequence. Instructions are issued beforehand and the competitors must complete the tests as indicated by cones, posts or markings. They are penalised for not performing any manoeuvre correctly; striking cones; failing to comply with the instructions; not attempting one or more of the components. There will also usually be time penalties.

Drag Racing: these are elimination events. They usually take place on disused airfields and the dragster cars are timed over a distance of 440 yards in pairs. The winner of each pair qualifies for the next round and so on.

Karting: at the top level, karts can attain speeds of more than 130 mph and provide all the excitement of circuit racing. Karts of up to 100cc can be raced by competitors over the age of 11.

Rallycross: this is faster and more professional than autocross. Multiple starts are normal and the circuit comprises both loose and sealed surfaces.

Rallying: to enter a rally you must join a club registered with the RAC's Motor Sport Division, who will put you in touch with the secretary of the nearest local club.